GEOFFREY BAWA

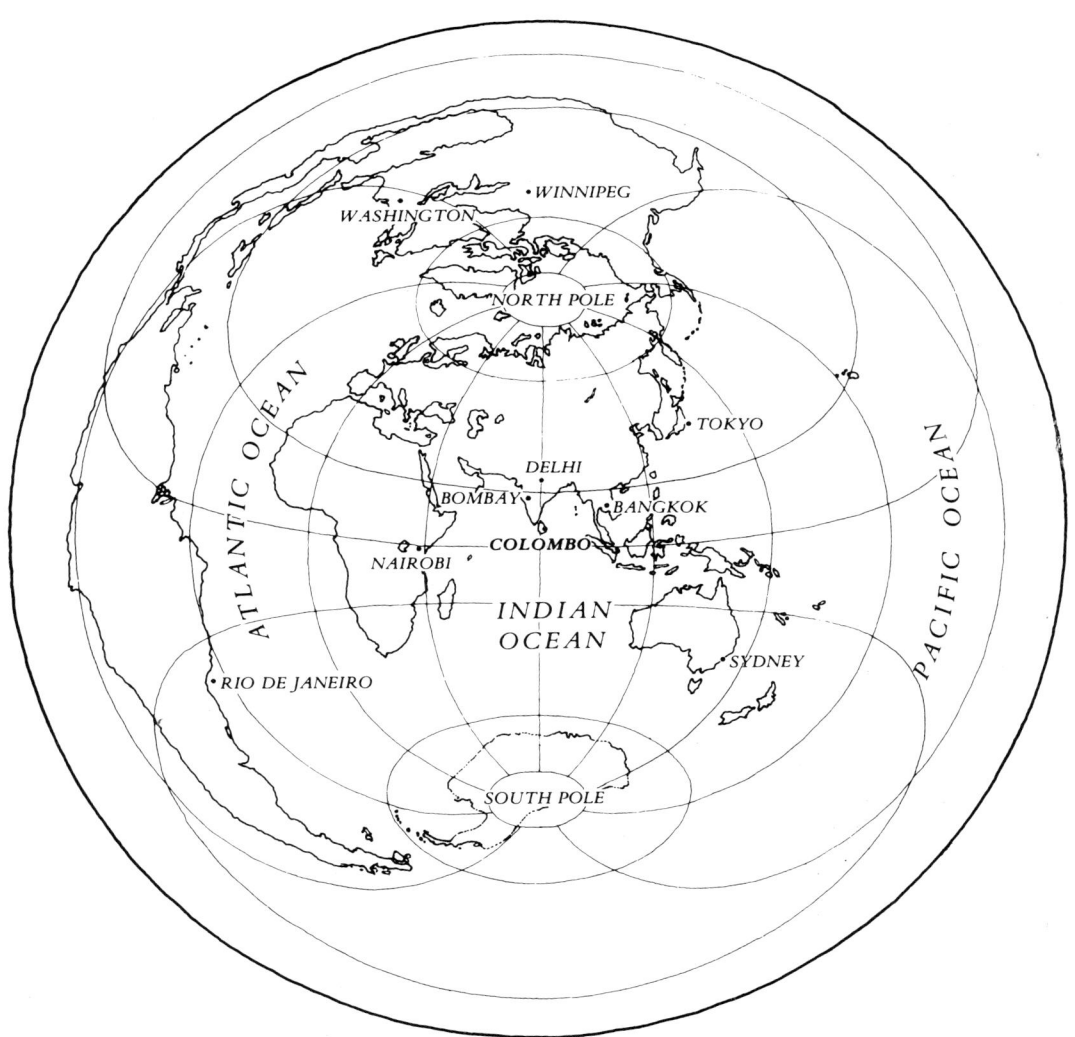

Map of the World centred on Colombo.

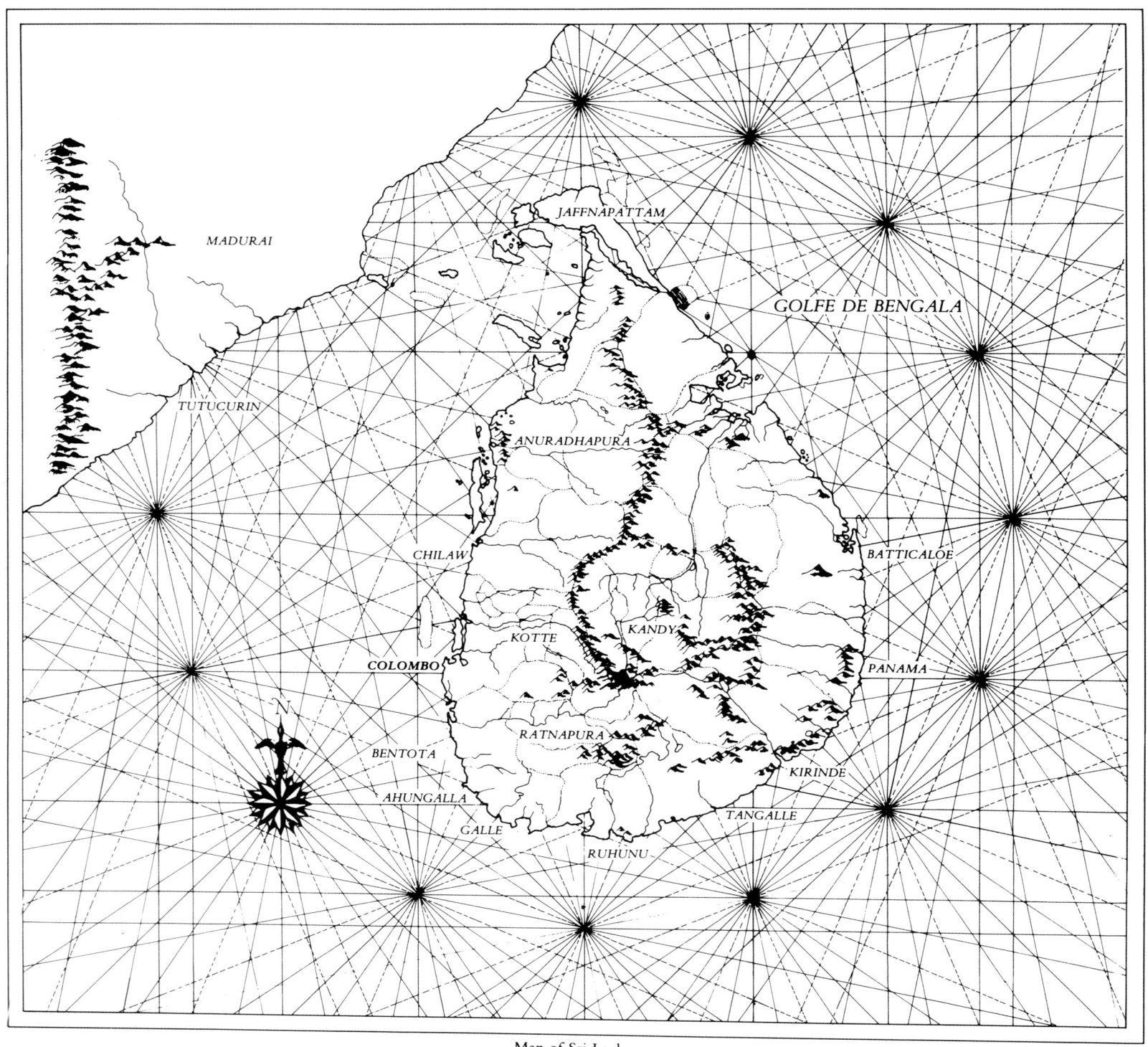

Map of Sri Lanka.

GEOFFREY BAWA

Revised edition

BRIAN BRACE TAYLOR

With an essay by Barbara Sansoni

THAMES AND HUDSON

Overleaf: Complete view of entrance facade and coconut-tree pool, Triton Hotel.

Photographs courtesy of Nihal Amarasinghe, Claire Henry Arni, Geoffrey Bawa, Christoph Bon, Richard Bryant, Priscilla Chenevix-Trench, Alan Gilbert, Martin Henry, H.U. Khan, Simon Laird, Mitsuo Matsuoka/Shinkenchiku, Milroy Perera, David Robson, Brian Brace Taylor, Hans Verbagh, Peter White and Rienzie Wijeratne.

In the new edition (1995) additional photographs are courtesy of Brian Brace Taylor, Channa Daswatte and Dominic Sansoni.

Photographs are the property of the photographers and may not be reproduced without their written permission. The drawings remain the property of the architect.

All drawings are courtesy of the architect Mr Geoffrey Bawa, who had them prepared especially for this book. Hunting Surveys (U.K.) photographed the drawings used in this publication, with the exception of the additional drawing used in the revised edition (1995), which is reproduced on p. 172 courtesy of Sumangala Jayatillaka.

Any copy of this book issued by the publisher as a paperback is sold subject to the condition that it shall not by way of trade or otherwise be lent, resold, hired out or otherwise circulated without the publisher's prior consent in any form of binding or cover other than that in which it is published and without a similar condition including these words being imposed on a subsequent purchaser.

This first paperback edition published in 1995
by Thames and Hudson Ltd, London
© 1986 and 1995 Geoffrey Bawa

All Rights Reserved. No part of this publication may be reproduced or transmitted in any form or by any means, electronic or mechanical, including photocopy, recording or any other information storage and retrieval system, without prior permission in writing from the publisher.

British Library Cataloguing-in-Publication Data

A catalogue record for this book is available from the British Library

ISBN 0-500-27858-X

Printed and bound in Italy by Contitipocolor

CONTENTS

9	A HOUSE IS A GARDEN Brian Brace Taylor	125	**HOTELS**
		126	BENTOTA BEACH HOTEL, BENTOTA
16	STATEMENT BY THE ARCHITECT Geoffrey Bawa	132	PANAMA HOTEL, PANAMA
		138	CLUB VILLA, BENTOTA
19	**GARDEN**	140	TRITON HOTEL, AHUNGALLA
		150	SERENDIB HOTEL, BENTOTA
20	THE GARDEN, LUNUGANGA with an essay by Ulrik Plesner		
		153	**PUBLIC BUILDINGS**
		154	CEYLON PAVILION EXPO 1970, OSAKA
45	**HOUSES**	156	MADURAI CLUB, SOUTHERN INDIA
46	ENA DE SILVA HOUSE, COLOMBO	162	SEEMA MALAKA, COLOMBO
50	THE ARCHITECT'S HOUSE, COLOMBO	164	NEW PARLIAMENTARY COMPLEX, SRI JAYA WARDENEPURA, KOTTE
58	STANLEY DE SARAM HOUSE, COLOMBO		
60	PETER WHITE HOUSE, MAURITIUS		
66	LIDIA GUNASEKERA HOUSE, BENTOTA	172	**RECENT WORK**
70	SUNETRA NANAYAKARA HOUSE, HORAGOLLA	174	KANDALAMA HOTEL, DAMBULLA
72	PAVILIONS, BATUJIMBAR, BALI	178	HOUSE ON THE CINNAMON HILL, LUNUGANGA, BENTOTA
81	**SCHOOLS**		
82	ST. BRIDGET'S MONTESSORI SCHOOL, COLOMBO	180	A BACKGROUND TO GEOFFREY BAWA Barbara Sansoni
84	YAHAPATH ENDERA FARM SCHOOL, HANWELLA	182	CHRONOLOGY OF WORKS
		189	BIOGRAPHY
92	INTEGRAL EDUCATION CENTRE, PILIYANDALA	189	BIBLIOGRAPHY
96	UNIVERSITY OF RUHUNU, MATARA ARTS AND SCIENCE FACULTIES		
113	**OFFICES**		
114	THE ARCHITECT'S OFFICE, COLOMBO		
120	STEEL CORPORATION OFFICE, ORUWELA		
122	AGRARIAN RESEARCH AND TRAINING INSTITUTE, COLOMBO		

PREFACE TO THE FIRST EDITION

I have been fortunate in the milieu in which I have worked. My engineer partner, Dr. Poologasundram, with his perceptive and intuitive understanding of building and of people, has been a strong supportive background against which imagination can play. Even at the start of a project, there is the knowledge that the intricacies of thought and organisation that ultimately lead to a finished building will be stabilised and directed. In all the buildings shown in this book he has been a prime participant. In the designing and building of Parliament, he frequently outcomputered the computers, adding just that fleck of brilliance that is in the human mind.

Obviously, in an architect's office one needs an enormous amount of help. We have again been fortunate. Vasantha Jacobsen, an architect of great sensitivity, has worked with us for many years, from the time she qualified. Apart from being involved in a number of projects, she was a major and constant prop in the building of Parliament. Other architects in the office include Stanley Perera, who has been there longer than I have, and Nihal Bodhinayake, who has had a continuous concern and care throughout the project for the building of the Ruhunu University. Two others are Ena de Silva and Laki Senanyake, both artists, both constant friends, and often participants in my work: neither ever fails in the understanding of a space or a feel for colour. Their personal work appears in some of the illustrations – the batik ceiling of the entrance to Bentota Beach Hotel, the painted ceiling of Parliament's arcade, the silver chandelier and the Triton Hotel murals.

It is not possible here to name everyone who has contributed to the finished buildings but there are many, some who have come and gone, and others who are still with us – both office staff and those on the site: head masons such as that pre-eminent Sahabdeen who, having looked at sixteenth scale drawings, understood precisely the entire idea of a project; carpenters and metal workers, co-ordinators and secretaries; and the hub of the turning wheel of my office, my secretary Janet.

GEOFFREY BAWA

PREFACE TO THE REVISED EDITION

I have since the publication of the earlier edition of this book continued to involve myself in a wide spectrum of work in Sri Lanka, India, Mauritius, Singapore and Fiji. The drawing boards in my home studio have carried designs for hotels and resorts, and private houses, as well as a lay-out for a botanic garden, some of which are included in this new edition.

More recently, the Kandalama Hotel has just been finished. This project, in the central part of Sri Lanka, is sited in an immensely beautiful setting overlooking an ancient lake. The construction has been managed by Milroy Perera and Deepal Wickramasinghe, whose collaboration was total. This spirit is visible also in the enthusiasm shown throughout by my assistants Dilshan Ferdinando, Sumangala Jayatillaka, Channa Daswatte and Amila de Mel.

GEOFFREY BAWA

ACKNOWLEDGMENTS FOR THE FIRST EDITION

Geoffrey Bawa is that rare architect whose work combines an environmentally appropriate beauty with a cultural sensitivity answering today's needs.

Brian Taylor, the author of this monograph, explored Bawa's work in Sri Lanka some three years ago for the Magazine *Mimar: Architecture in Development*. In the course of writing the article, he became excited about the possibilities of a book, but for a number of reasons was unable to follow up on it immediately. A year later, at about the same time that *Mimar*'s editors had begun to pursue the book idea, we learned that the Royal Institute of British Architects in London was planning an exhibition of Bawa's work. Both of these projects took shape aided by two of Bawa's architect friends in London (who insist they remain anonymous). They were the ones who forced the busy architect to sit down with us and select the materials, which they coordinated and organised into presentation form. This book owes much – possibly its existence – to their efforts.

During the year that we were working on the book we were assisted by a number of people who also believed that Bawa's work deserved greater recognition – to all of whom we are grateful; here we can only name a few. C. Anjalandran in Colombo not only researched Bawa's work carefully, but also provided the author with many insights. Dominic Sansoni, Milroy Pereira, Barbara Sansoni, and others also added greatly to our knowledge of the subject. The several photographers provided us with marvellous images. Mitsui of Japan were generous in their provision of photographs and information. Hunting Surveys and Consultants in London meticulously reproduced the line drawings specially prepared by Geoffrey Bawa's office.

The "in-house" team's role was of course paramount in the effort. Brian Taylor not only wrote the text but also coordinated the publication; in the latter he was assisted by Marie-Odile Benard in Paris. Concept Media's staff, especially Patricia Theseira and the designers from Viscom Design Associates, Sylvia Tan and Ko Hui Huy, lavished their care and attention on the work above and beyond the call of duty. Finally, all of us involved in the effort are proud to play a part in bringing Geoffrey Bawa the wider international attention he deserves. This book celebrates the emergence of a major architectural voice.

HASAN-UDDIN KHAN
SERIES EDITOR, MIMAR BOOKS

A HOUSE IS A GARDEN

Brian Brace Taylor

Geoffrey Bawa was initially — and I gather still is — deeply reticent about any attempt to put words next to the reality of what he has created, namely the architecture and garden designs shown in this book. I share that reticence, but for different reasons: as a non-Sri Lankan, and as a historian who has not sufficiently seen, analysed and reflected upon the rich cultural heritage of ancient Ceylon, it is perhaps presumptuous on my part to venture forward against our respective misgivings. Yet it is impossible to pass through/over Bawa's artistic production in silence; a few guideposts are needed, which I shall offer, and the reader must then judge, on the basis of first impressions taken from the printed images — like myself from brief, although first-hand, encounters with the reality — whether my appreciations aid in understanding the significance of the work.

Two essential factors manifest themselves above all others in the built work of Geoffrey Bawa, time and geography. Some years ago the Mexican poet Octavio Paz gave a lecture of which I am reminded entitled "The New Analogy", and said the following:

"Every society possesses what is called an 'image of the world'. This image has its roots in the unconscious structure of society and requires a specific conception of time to foster it. The works and words of men are made of time, they are time: they are a movement towards this or that, whatever the reality the this or that designates, even if it is nothingness itself. Time is the depository of meaning".[1]

Paz then proceeds to give examples of Greek time, Christian time, Hindu time, and ultimately, Modern time, in order to demonstrate how different were the 'world images' at those moments of history. The modern age was (because we are at the end of it) an "age of criticism", says the poet; now we are standing at the threshold of a new era. It is a synchronic view of time, and as Barbara Sansoni points out in her essay, Sri Lanka has known many of these "times" throughout her long and rich cultural history.

For our purposes in trying to understand Bawa's production as an architect, it is useful to keep in mind that Bawa is very much a man of the end of the modern era — especially when seen the context of the modern movement in the West — because he was trained abroad, is widely-read and widely travelled. In short, he is highly cosmopolitan: he knows what is going on elsewhere in the world, culturally-speaking. Yet, there is of course a diachronic interpretation of his work, of his own development and its specificity in relation to Sri Lanka. So, on the one hand, it seems to me, there is the Geoffrey Bawa whose emergence professionally coincides with the break-up of the modern movement in the late 1950's and early 1960's, and on the other hand, Geoffrey Bawa who transposes these concerns, among them a search for new "vitality and validity", to the Sri Lankan scene.

Besides the element of time, or history, which is basic to Bawa's architecture, there is the central role of geography. His conception of a building, nearly all of his buildings, is strongly influenced by the character of the natural terrain, the vegetation, the potential for developing vistas out onto the landscape, and hence, light and shade; and of course, the related and ever present aspect of climate. This quality which pervades Bawa's work, of passionate concern for an architecture that is in and of the landscape, is discernible first and foremost in his own garden at Lunuganga, then in his private houses, institutional and hotel buildings. Rarely do his designs allow the architecture to pre-empt the primordial importance of the natural surroundings, either by their scale, use of materials, or siting; an exception to this is perhaps the Parliamentary complex. On the other hand, the Ruhunu university project (see elevations) is an excellent recent example of constructions that are tied intimately to the topography and the territory they occupy.

Architects, like poets, musicians, and painters, all have their points of departure on an artistic itinerary, and each has his or her own points of reference, like cairns, along the way. Living architects are generally loath to speak about these, especially when the influences are of the recent past. Bawa is no exception, and while he may be cajoled into talking about Italian gardens of the 16th century, it is left to the historian and critic to situate his work within the context of architecture over the last twenty-five years, for example.

Architecture of the so-called "heroic" period of the modern movement came to an end around 1960; that is to

---

[1] "The New Analogy", Cooper Union, N.Y., 1972, p. 3).

GEOFFREY BAWA

Perspective view of Lunuganga garden and lodgings, representing the configuration of outdoor 'rooms' in 1985.
Drawing by Philip Fowler.

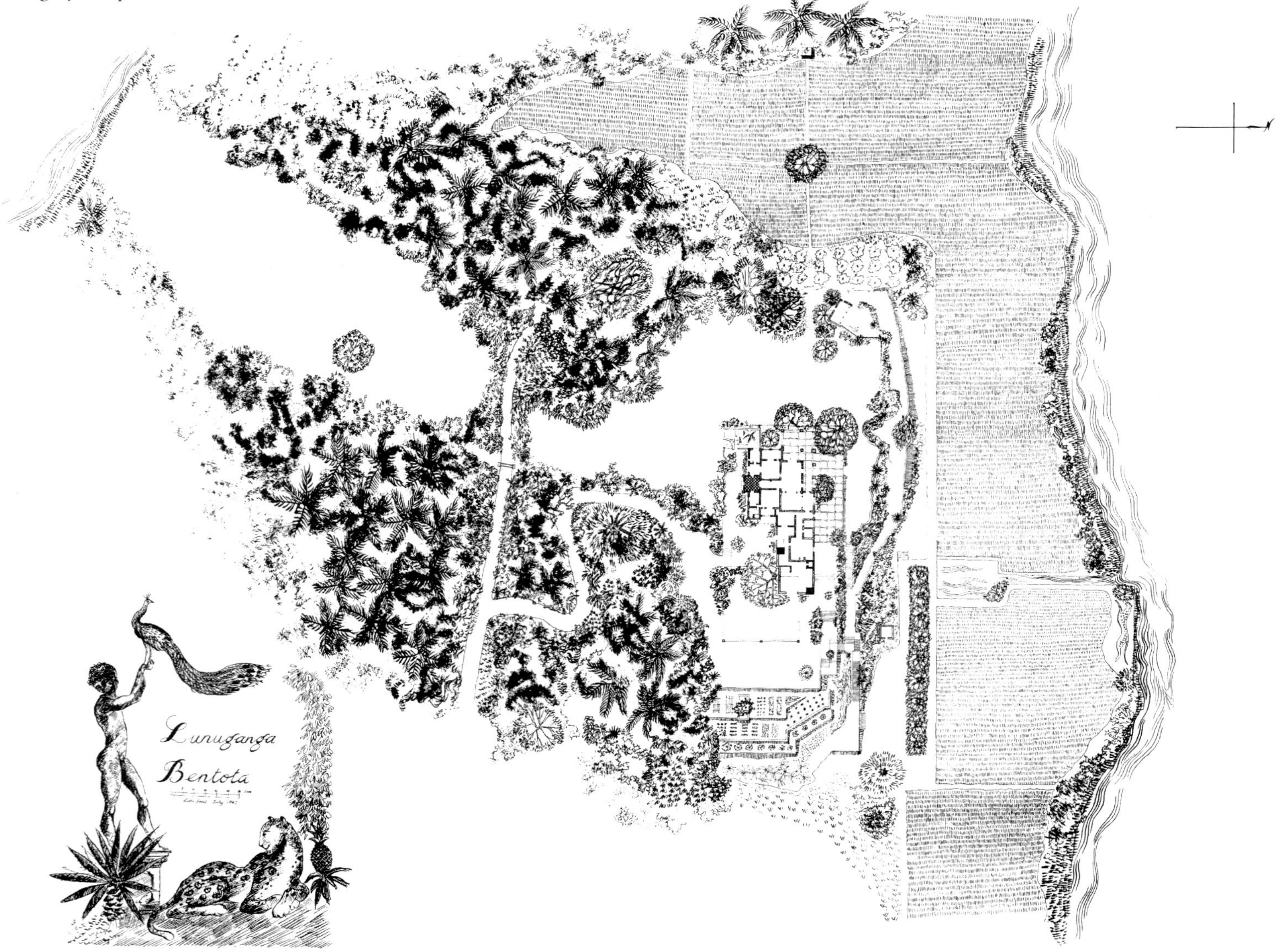

Plan of the garden and house at Lunuganga in July, 1962, approximately 12 years after it was begun. (Cf. plan of 1983).
Drawing by Laki Senanyake.

say, the image of the world fostered by the members of C.I.A.M., with Le Corbusier at its head, did in turn begin to be criticised, and it is one of the valid reasons why Bawa's world should not, cannot be understood without taking this fact into account. He finished his architectural studies in England in the late 1950's, precisely when a post war generation (e.g. Team 10, etc.) was challenging the doctrines instituted by their predecessors — and was moreover called into question by the appearance of uncanonical buildings such as Ronchamp chapel or the Jaoul and Sarabhai houses. Indeed, one should recall that was the period of Aldo van Eyck's enthusiastic studies of Dogon settlements in Africa, and his own subsequent project for a new type of orphanage in Amsterdam, De Carlo's Urbino Campus and the early works of Americans Louis Kahn, Charles Moore and Robert Venturi. Bawa, certainly aware of all these new trends began his own career when he was nearly 40 years old and, conceivably, was less prone to idolatry or passing fads of a purely stylistic nature. Allusions to history, to numerous histories became acceptable again.

This is not to say that his earliest buildings when first associated with Edwards, Reid and Begg did not reflect contemporary western models of structure, materials and detailing. They did: his office building for the automobile association, St. Thomas' school extension and the Bishop's college classrooms employed exposed reinforced concrete in an explicit manner. Cantilevers, concrete relief decoration, beams in concrete carried forward to the facade, and so forth, testify both to his training and mostly likely to certain clients' tastes. The architecture of these institutional buildings begins to be inflected towards a more personal vocabulary in the Montessori school in 1964.

In domestic designs, where most architects first reveal themselves anyway, Bawa's house for A.S.H. de Silva at Galle (1960) is curiously modernist and traditional at the same time: in plan, it recalls the pin-wheel layout of Mies van der Rohe's brick country house (1923), yet at the very heart of the house (almost as Wright would have put the chimney there) our architect has placed a planted court, fountain and pool. However, what is most significant are the relationships established with the geography of the terrain and the garden. The section drawing reveals a single extended roof that

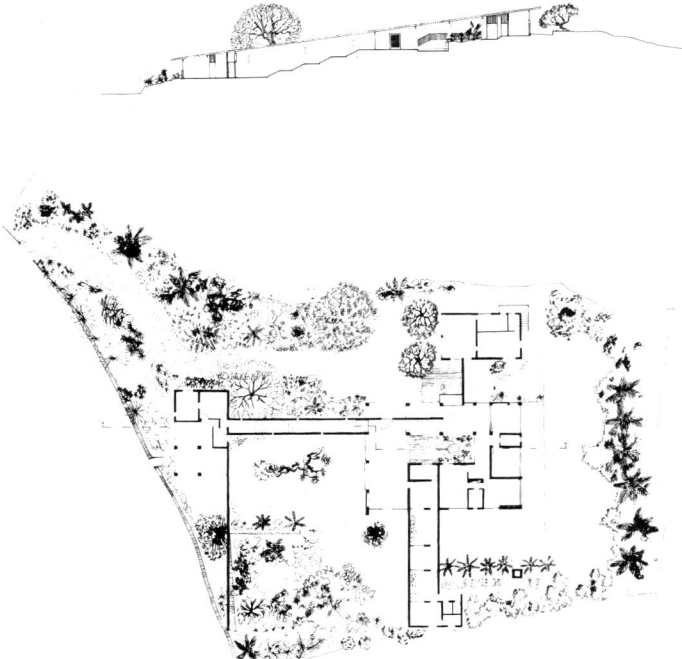

Plan and section of A.S.H. De Silva house, 1960.

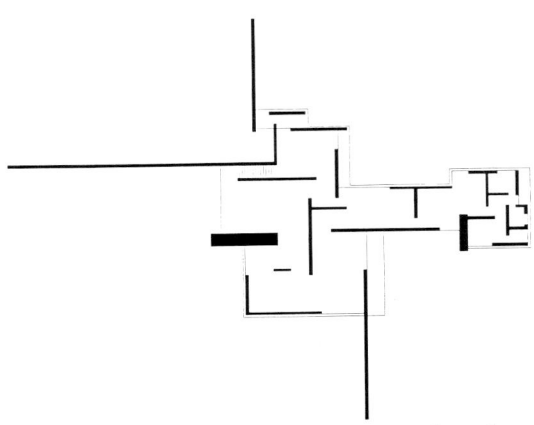

Plan of a projected country house. Mies van der Rohe, architect, 1923.

Ames Gate House, North Easton, Massachusetts, U.S.A. H.H. Richardson, architect, 1883.

Elevation of the Beruwana estate owner's residence, project by G. Bawa in 1967.

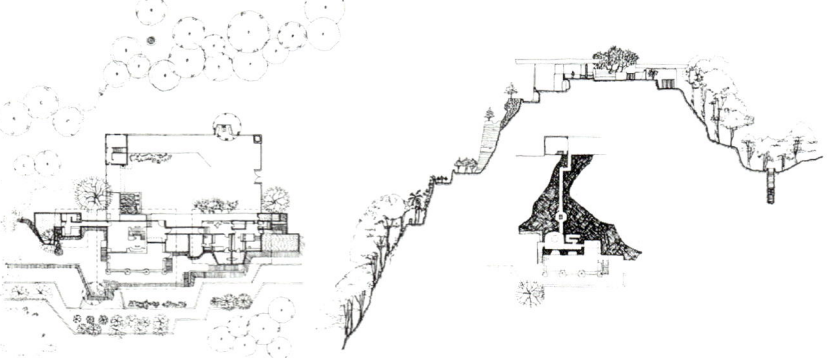

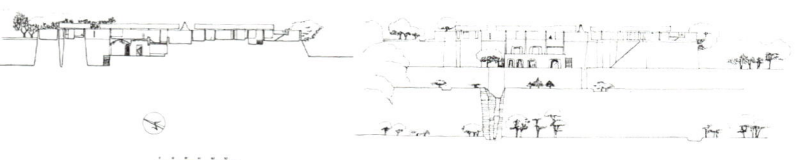

Section of the Beruwana estate house, 1967.

follows the slope, from lower office entrance to upper living quarters, in one continuous line. This gesture, of an all encompassing expression of shelter, seems to signal the architect's tentative search for an appropriate image of dwelling place, in perfect sympathy with the environment.

The other dwellings from this early phase of Bawa's career reveal impulses to which he was subsequently to give free rein and which leads us into his very personal world where distinctions between what is man-made and that produced by nature become fused. In 1967, he planned out in collaboration with architect Ulrik Plesner, and the client himself, on the very site itself a projected bungalow (not illustrated in this book) nestled among, around, on top of giant boulders at the Polontalawa estate. Again, the impetus was apparently to integrate liveable space and natural setting — at the most extreme limits imaginable. Parallels with American architect H.H. Richardson's Ames Gate House, constructed of huge uncut stones taken from the very site comes to mind, as do others by Wright or even C.N. Ledoux. The bungalow signifies more than a search for ultimate origins, the primitive hut so to speak; it is space, a room(s), encompassing nature. It defies historical categories, creates a *tabula rasa*. The second project (unbuilt) was the Beruwana Estate house, perched atop a steep terraced hillside. Both section and elevation underscore the architect's urge to design an abode which also merges with the landscape to provide an ideal harmony between shelter and terrain. These projects reveal an undercurrent in Bawa's architecture that becomes a predominant force in his method of approach to solving new commissions, of all types in subsequent years. They are pivotal in what becomes a passionate quest for a language involving nature (or geography) and history (or time) and Bawa's own capacity for synthesis.

However much one accepts the parallels with Bawa's 18th or 19th century predecessors abroad who, at a particular moment in time sought the sources of new, *authentic* architecture, local history in Sri Lanka (political, social and cultural) acted unequivocally as a catalyser in Bawa's formulation of an expressive language all his own. The policies of Mrs. Bandaranaike as leader of Sri Lanka in the late 1950's expressed independence and self-reliance in all fields, with the result of a considerable amount of introspection on the cultural level. Bawa's close friends and associates, Laki Senanyake, Barbara Sansoni, Plesner and others spent much time renewing or extending their knowledge of traditional building, monumental and vernacular, the materials, techniques, symbols and functions. Ena de Silva, world renowned for her *batik* designs, was of this same artistic milieu and it was she who commissioned Bawa to do a house for her and her husband in 1962. While the architect admits that Ena de Silva made very clear what she desired, he also claims that "it was the first time I could really design a house for someone else as though I was doing it for myself". The dialogue was exceptional, and the house that resulted is a blend of modern sensibilities and traditional elements.

Much of what has been written previously on Bawa's architecture refers constantly to its inspiration from local vernacular building — its being a contemporary interpretation of course, of these traditions. While the Ena de Silva house, Bawa's own offices begun in 1963, and his Colombo house commencing in 1969, with their interior courtyards, colonnaded passageways, and clay tile roofs each demonstrate a personal change in Bawa's vocabulary from his earliest beginnings, to categorise them as 'vernacular' is to dismiss them, and hence to disregard the significant overlays of historical knowledge embodied in each one. Tradition is present, to one degree or another, in Bawa's work but there are *many* sources, some local, many from faraway cultures and times. In this sense, his architecture is paradoxical: it is uncontestably Sri Lankan, but at the same time it is not. As we said earlier, Bawa has been producing at the *end* of one era (modern time) and the beginning of another: his contemporaries elsewhere in the world with whom one sees affinities in attitude towards their work emanating from the 1960's, are the Robert Venturi of *Complexity and Contradiction in Architecture* (NYC, 1965) and the Charles Moore of the MLTW houses in California of that period — to cite but one positive trend. At home in Sri Lanka, one must mention the early buildings of architect Minnette De Silva, which although they reveal a somewhat similar cross-fertilisation of traditional with Western vocabulary, they are of an entirely different spirit than Bawa's.

Take for example Bawa's total restructuring of the rowhouses on 33rd Lane that progressively became his

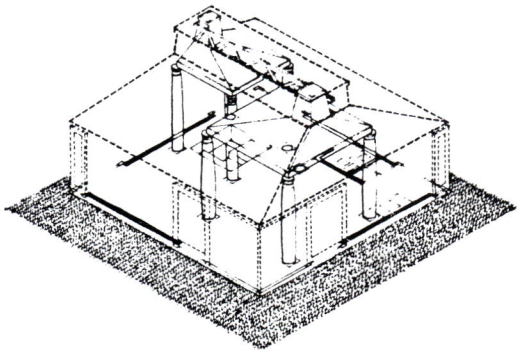

Axonometric of the Charles Moore weekend house, Orinda, California, 1961. *Aediculae* are used to create spatial areas within the total volume of the house.

The *dana salarwa*, reception building on the estate of Maha Kappina Walauwa where Buddhist monks periodically came to receive food from the owner.

View of bridge connecting portions of the Castel Vecchio museum in Verona, Italy by Carlo Scarpa.

Mouth of Hell sculpture in the park of the Villa Orsini in Italy.

Mask of a Hindu Pan in the Lunuganga garden.

Colombo residence. Set in an urban milieu, the architect remapped the interior 'geography' of the houses, introducing a multitude of internal courtyards, lightwells, pools, construction elements salvaged from elsewhere, to achieve a succession of carefully composed *vistas* comparable to his garden at Lunuganga, but on a more intimate and confined scale. For me, the house is a metaphor for a garden. The spirit which permeates it is the same, the manipulation of space and objects in that space is similar. His antique Rolls Royce in pristine shape at the garage entrance is not the Apollo statue of the garden (although their mutual displacement in time and in culture are noteworthy), nor is the settee in front of the Rolls the bench of the garden's summer pavilion, but the wilful artifice and the irony behind the combination of such objects to be contemplated is significant.

A unique and modernist quality of Bawa's architecture is his *redeploying* of components, salvaged ancient artifacts, columns, a window or a jar, in newly circumscribed contexts. The demolition and reconstruction of one of the houses in the Lydia Gunasekera compound is typical of this strategy. Taking the paradigm of the fortress for example, Bawa embroiders upon the shape and the entrance passage of this local historic building-type from the former Portuguese and Dutch invaders and in the Bentota Beach hotel turns the model inside out as it were, placing continuous, cantilevered, open galleries all around the exterior One archetypal element which is constantly redeployed in Bawa's buildings, comparable to the *aedicula* in Charles Moore's early houses, is the *dana salarwa*, a traditional, long, colonnaded room open on both sides and devoted uniquely to periodic offering of food to assembled Buddhist monks. Similarly, at Batujimbar gardens in Bali, the unachieved project depended upon local technology and materials, to be sure, yet the incorporation by the architect of historical artifacts or other vestiges of an ancient culture, and the landscape itself, into each different pavilion reflects a sophisticated 20th-century interpretation; call it poetic licence.

In his approach to, or reactions to, the artifacts of those civilisations to which he is closest, Bawa's architecture is analogous to that of the late Italian designer Carlo Scarpa. Each operated in a cultural milieu, Venice and Ceylon, that abounds with layers of successive 'images of the world',

View from the pavilion — the garden as a "series of rooms"...

where Oriental and Western traditions are intermingled. There exists in the work of both artists a measure of *collage*, of a very refined sort, whereby references to the past are given legitimacy previously excluded from modern architecture. Theirs is what we might call a revisionist approach, allowing for overt, explicit, citation of sources, even from the modern masters like Wright or Aalto. Finally, the method of working of both Bawa and Scarpa is worth mentioning, since both belong to the myth of the architect who can never seem to finish a drawing completely and provide it to the builder for execution, the trauma of Bawa's life was having to work with a Japanese construction firm for the new Parliamentary complex, where tight schedules had to be met and few changes could be made as one went along. Scarpa was notorious for ultimately having to relinquish a drawing to an assistant for completion and transmital to the builder; moreover, modifying details on the site, to the construction or to the landscape, is a trait shared by both men. The parallels are intended simply to invoke their appurtanance to a generation whose architecture reflects a multitude of conscious references to the past, comprehensible ingredients of an increasingly 'universal vocabulary', frequently cross-cultural in nature, and assimilated into a revised architectural syntax. New meanings emerge.

We began this essay by alluding to Bawa's garden at Lunuganga as providing a necessary key to penetrate the substance and significance of his architecture. It is a secluded world, (here made public in this book for the first time in all its splendour) yet its source of inspiration takes us back again to Italy — but this time to the 16th century and not the 20th — to the garden of Bomarzo near Viterbo by Vicino Orsini, begun in 1552. The complexity of the iconographic programme of the Bomarzo garden, often symbolised by the Hell Mouth carved from the living rock, would have been understood by a limited group of friends, ... and humanists well-versed in Italian literature and thought from Dante through Ludovico Ariosto[2]. Bawa at Lunuganga has developed a much less literary, allegorical programme. Nonetheless, his inclusion of a "Plain of Jars" (Plateau of the Vases at Bomarzo), a giant mask of a Hindu Pan (sculpted Heads and Masks in Orsini's garden), the Apollo-like statue and stone leopard, and his opening up of a vista to the *dagoba* temple (Templetto at Bomarzo) are specific features linking Bawa to this Humanist tradition. Lunuganga is not a copy of Bomarzo, for there are other antecedents present also, but a transposition of the concept into an altered context and time. The older allegorical presentations serve Bawa's investigation into contemporary configurations of image and pure sensation, or feeling.

The garden, says Bawa, "is a series of rooms seen in succession or as a whole". His buildings are qualitatively inseparable from this vision of time and geography. The architect and landscapist are one and the same; he projects a path of vision, deploys objects, contains spaces, arranges light and shadow across a vast or a constrained geographical tableau. Bawa's most successful works, be they self-contained introverted houses or the extended university complex at Ruhunu, are the creation of places for vistas onto Nature. It may be a view of roofscapes from above the double pitched, clay tile roofs towards the southern horizon, or the *trompe l'oeil* sequence of pools whose relationships in reality are left ironically ambiguous, as at the approach to the Triton Hotel.

One relevant definition of time we have neglected thus far is perennial or seasonal change. We have mentioned various frameworks for relating Bawa's designs to the past, but there is also now, and then the future, with cyclical change. The connivance of climate and natural vegetation in Sri Lanka renders the garden an enchanting but everchanging phenomenon, fragile in existence, even ephemeral in the face of natural forces. Buildings in Sri Lanka (southern India, Indonesia) by Geoffrey Bawa will succumb to the same destiny one senses, after he has finished with them, as the garden. This is not unique to his architecture — it applies to any — but the process is accelerated under these particular conditions and times. Whether they are built symbols of political power and prestige, of a faith in education, or beautiful metaphorical allusions to past cultures, Bawa's architecture epitomises an indissoluble bond between *image* and *sensations* of the permanance or the passing of time. The garden is an emblem for the abode and the abode for a garden.

---

[2] Darnale, M.J. and Weil, M.S. "Il Sacro Bosco Di Bomarzo: Its 16th Century Literary and Antiquarian Context". Journal of Garden History, Vol. 4, No. 1, III, Jan — Mar 1984.

STATEMENT BY THE ARCHITECT

In my personal search I have been aware of the past — many periods of the past: Medieval Italian hill towns with their splendid instinctive massing of buildings which although varied in purpose and age make a magnificent total picture; great English country houses and their essential complement of park and garden; Greek, Roman, Mexican and Buddhist ruins, the Alhambra in Granada, the chapel in Ronchamps, the Mogul forts in Rajasthan, and the marvellous palace of Padmanabapuram. There are so many instances when my eye was caught by a landscape, a small unimportant but beautiful building, or a large and splendid one, sometimes seen for a moment from a swiftly moving car or train, for a day or two, or sometimes lived amongst, like the buildings in Cambridge and Rome. The beauty of some of these buildings, gardens and landscapes leaves a considerable residue of subconscious understanding in the mind — a help to solve some present need; for the right placement of a building on the site; for the need to frame and emphasise a view or to open or construct a space; a wish to get a definite degree of light or shadow in a room. Good building in Sri Lanka has always taken these into account from the temples, monasteries and palaces of Anuradhapura, Polonnaruwa, Sigiriya and its water garden and all the other buildings that followed through the ages to the present day. I like to regard all past and present good architecture in Sri Lanka as just that — good Sri Lankan architecture — for this is what it is, not narrowly classified as Indian, Portuguese or Dutch, early Sinhalese or Kandyan or British Colonial, for all the good examples of these periods have taken the country itself into first account.

When you look at the better examples of what remains of these earlier buildings you find they all have met the essentials of life in Sri Lanka, but although the past gives lessons it does not give the whole answer to what must be done now. It is true that many of the materials available to us are the same as in the past, and their use — if sensible and right — very alike except where new techniques have added to or changed their qualities. With these and other new materials we must now design for a society living in a framework of a difficult economy, a much faster life — sometimes a freer one — new conventions and a greater liberality of belief to all the dictates of ever-changing needs. But there is, against this background of life, the great constant of the climate.

One unchanging element of all buildings is the roof — protective, emphatic, and all important — governing the aesthetic whatever the period, wherever the place. Often a building is only a roof, columns and floors — the roof dominant, shielding, giving the contentment of shelter. Ubiquitous, pervasively present, the scale or pattern shaped by the building beneath. The roof, its shape, texture and proportion is the strongest visual factor.

At random I take an isolated item, the — what is now called — Sinhala tile. The Arab traders introduced to Sri Lanka many centuries ago the half-round clay roofing tile of the Mediterranean world, but the roofs built in Sri Lanka with them

STATEMENT BY THE ARCHITECT

Painting by Donald Friend.

were more steeply pitched to shed the huge rainfall of our country. The Portuguese and the Dutch used the same tile and roof pitch but the latter raised the roofs higher for coolness, with wide eaves and verandahs to shade the walls. In the hill country the Kandyans used a flat clay tile like a shingle on their double-pitched roofs in meeting halls which had only columns, no walls — an answer to a way of life — a great roof to give shade and shelter, open to the drift of air and the encompassing view. More than functional building it is first rational building, for it is rational to give presence to both function and form, to admit beauty and pleasure as well as purpose.

These are my basic thoughts but there are many more: thoughts on details; the proportions of rooms, doors and windows; the heights, the sweeps and pitches of roofs; where one looks from a room, at what, and through what, at what is to be seen; how open or closed a view from a room should be. In these considerations no rules can guide, or if they could, would not always give exactly the right answer. It is in this realm of part emotion part thought, that the rest of the way must run, and it is at this stage that the architect steps, from the relative security of known and learnt things, into the world of intuition, inspiration, talent, gift — call it what you will, a world inside his head and far outside it at the same time — almost sub- or super-conscious. This may seem extravagant when written down but it is the unknown factor. I suppose it is here that each one of us has a separate and personal impulse — the point at which, although surrounded by the fact and reality of a project, one is alone and must make a decision to do this and not that, to do what seems at the moment inevitable.

The buildings shown on the following pages illustrate, as far as drawings and photographs can, the architectural answers I have found to a variety of needs. For myself a building can only be understood by moving around and through it and by experiencing the modulation and feel of the spaces one moves through — from the outside into verandahs, then rooms, passages, courtyards — the view from these spaces into others, views through to the landscape beyond, and from outside the building, views back through rooms into inner rooms and courts. Equally important, the play of light in both garden and inner room — from a shaded inner space to the celebration of light in a courtyard. To archieve the possibility of enjoyment and pleasure is so necessary, in addition to comfort and functional use. When one delights as much as I do in planning a building and having it built I find it impossible to describe the exact steps in an analytical or dogmatic way. Every project is different, and each approach, each individual design based on the differing backgrounds of site and purpose, requires a separate and total involvement and a care that must extend from the foundations of the structures to the smallest detail of the ultimate furnishing of rooms.

I have touched on a variety of points that have occurred to me which might be useful in helping to understand my buildings but I have a very strong conviction that it is impossible to explain architecture in words — I have always enjoyed seeing buildings but seldom enjoyed reading explanations about them — as I feel, with others, that architecture cannot be totally explained but must be experienced.

GARDEN
THE GARDEN, LUNUGANGA

THE GARDEN, LUNUGANGA

A small rubber plantation consisting of a house and 25 acres of land was purchased in 1949. There was a low hill planted with rubber and fruit trees and coconut palms, with rice fields at the lower level, the whole surrounded by the Dedduwa Lake. This lake is a backwater of the Bentota River and has an island in it of almost the same area as the Lunuganga promontary. The island is a bird sanctuary and has never been lived on, at least certainly since the 13th century where it was used as a burial place for priests of the temples nearby.

When Geoffrey Bawa bought the promontary, it had a dwelling that became the core of the present house, which continues to receive additions. The thick plantations of rubber trees surrounding the house when it was bought made it impossible to perceive the lake from even the higher ground and the house itself. The felling of trees on a selective basis and the changing of land forms were the start of the making of a garden. The house itself was extensively altered, terraces were built, and through the years continuous change both to the building and the garden, has made them as they are now. Most of the planting, both trees and shrubs, has been done since 1950. It is an ongoing process. The garden is shown in its present state.

View of the garden with statue and Temple tree in blossom.

Vista to the south towards the *dagoba* from the house at Lunuganga.

GARDEN

Plan of the house and garden in 1985.

LUNUGANGA

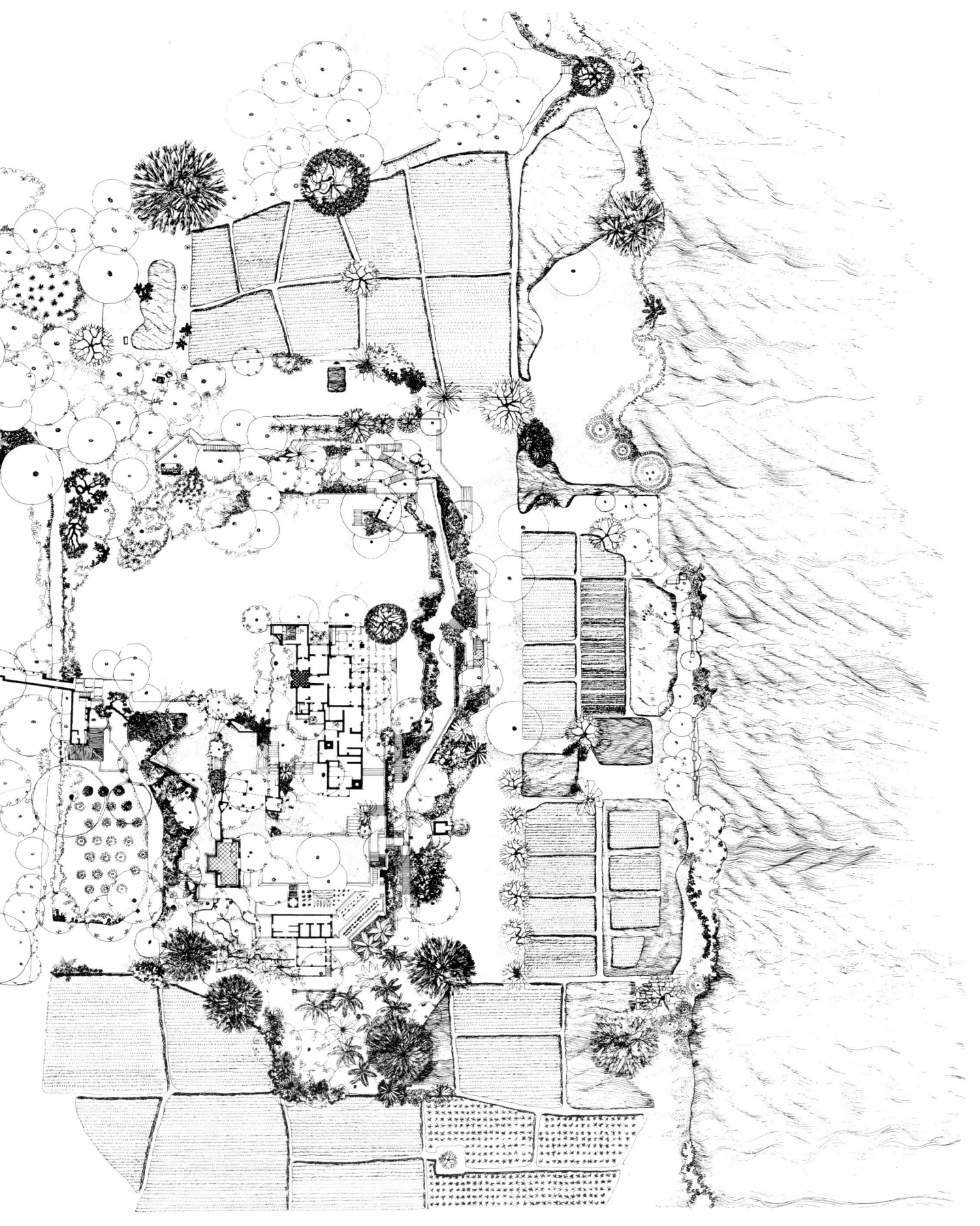

GARDEN

Twisted trees at entrance steps to the house.

Entrance steps and colonnaded portico.

View of entrance terrace from a verandah.

Terrace and entry to the house.

Western end of the entrance terrace.

LUNUGANGA

View from the front door towards the distant *dagoba* (temple).

View of the entry and hallway from the drawing room.

Drawing room seen from the dining room.

The verandah looking towards the lagoon.

The Temple tree

GARDEN

The watergate (foreground) and lagoon from the upper terrace.

Looking northward across the watergate.

View westward from the upper terrace with statue.

LUNUGANGA

View westward with mask of a Hindu Pan.

Summer house in the garden seen from the north.

GARDEN

Sectional elevation of the house and its recent extensions.

South facade of the house with front door.

South facade.

Grove of trees leading down to the 'Plain of Jars'.

GARDEN

Pool and 'Plain of Jars' looking towards the blue pavilion.

Three arecanut palms, three jars and pool.

A well and kumbuk tree.

Detail of the blue pavilion.

Sculpted mask of a Hindu Pan.

GARDEN

Paddy, balustrade and lagoon.

Statue of a leopard and the trees at lagoon's edge.

Central stairway leading to the middle-level walk from lower broad walk.

View towards western stairway and 'Plain of Jars'.

Overleaf: View of eastern end of the broad walk and upper garden.

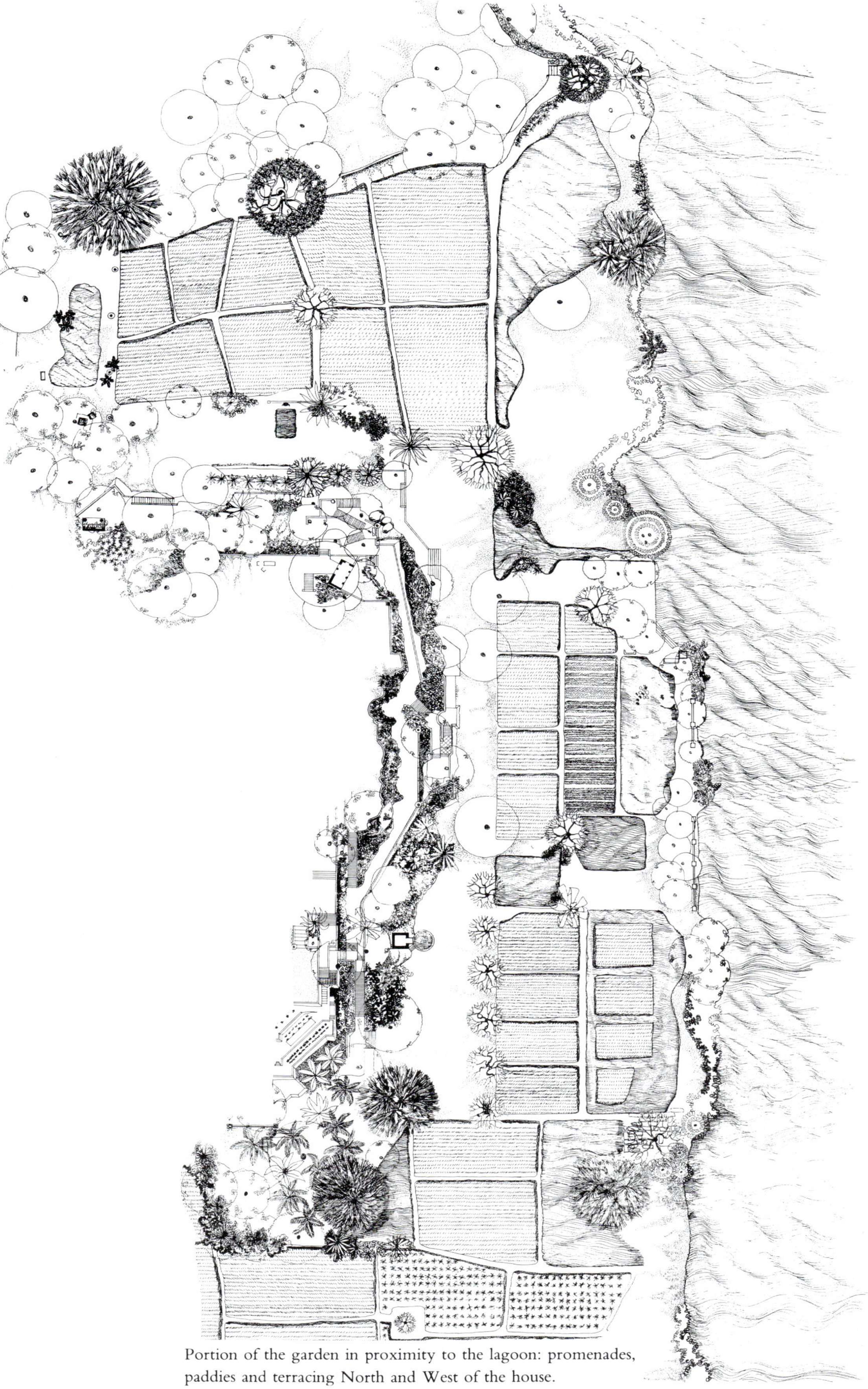

Portion of the garden in proximity to the lagoon: promenades, paddies and terracing North and West of the house.

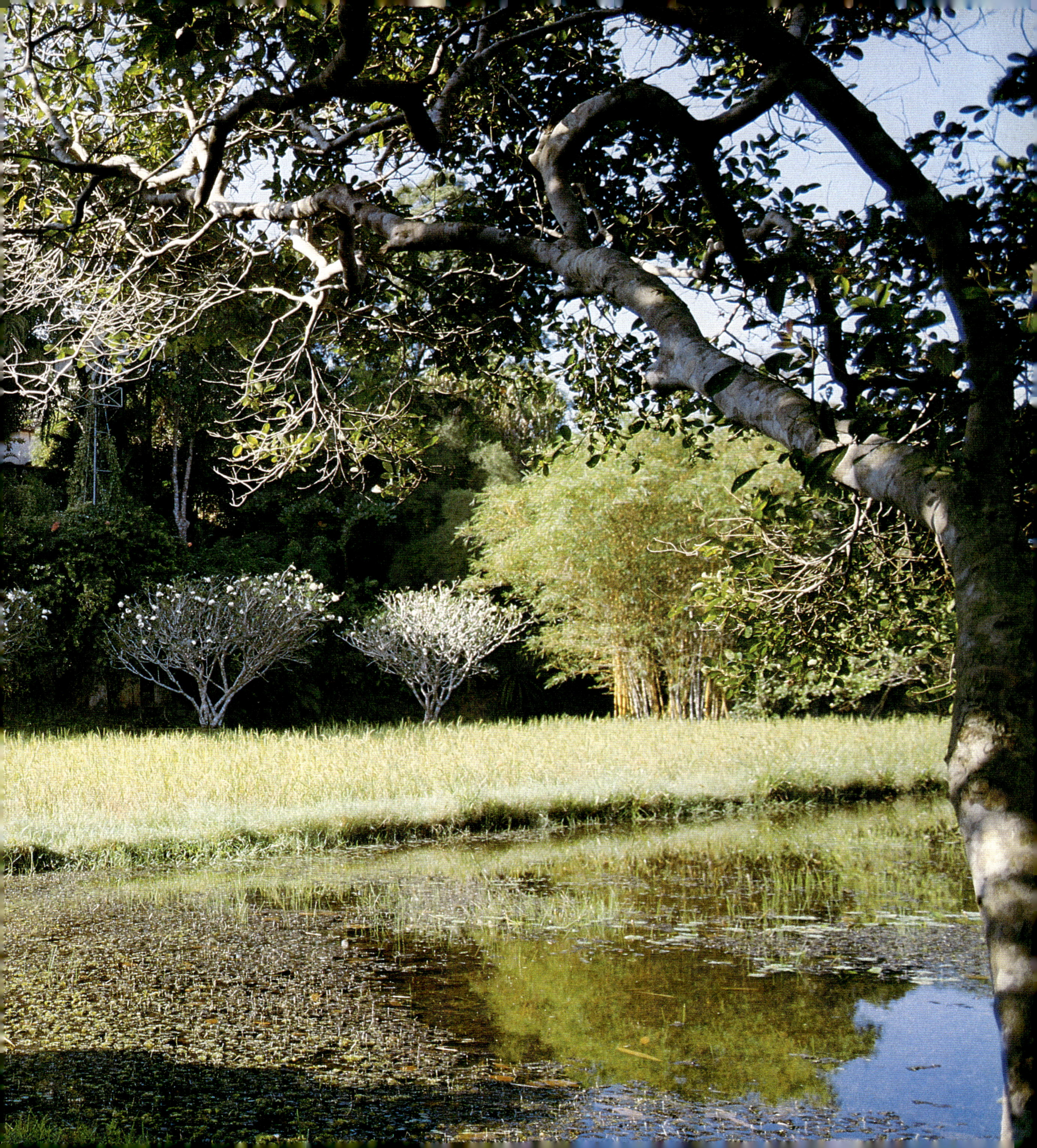

GARDEN

Plan of the pavilion, hen house, and adjacent landscaping, in 1983.

LUNUGANGA

Looking back from the viewpoint towards the house and pavilion.

Hen house.

Blue doors of the pavilion extension to the house.

GARDEN

Interior of the pavilion.

Interior of the pavilion.

View into the pavilion from the entrance portico.

View through the portico, with bedroom above, to entrance court.

GARDEN

Sunset from the upper terrace.

A TEN-YEAR-OLD GARDEN IN CEYLON

Ulrik Plesner

Ceylon is a cone-shaped island. In the centre are high steaming mountains, with waterfalls and rivers and wild vegetation, broken by plantations of closely arranged, bluegreen tea bushes between which the earth shines scarlet. On the lower slopes, the sky is reflected in the flooded paddy fields which, like an enormous glass-staircase in a baroque fantasy, lead down to the lowlands by the coast. The paddy fields are flooded one-third of the year from large artificial lakes, many of which were constructed by the Ceylonese kings about the year 500 A.D. The paddy fields weave through the jungle of the lowlands like large lakes. The undergrowth along the edges leans out with leaves that vary from quite small to over four metres in length. Houses only three metres from the edge are invisible. Everything grows quickly and juicely. If you put a stick in the ground, it sprouts leaves and roots the next day. I have taken a clump of bamboos twice the height of a two-storey house, dragged it two kilometres on the road by a lorry and planted it by a new house and two weeks later it was healthy. If you sow a plant you must step aside at once.

For a year now I have followed a garden being made. In Denmark gardens require patience. We let ours grow and cut paths. There are too many dull years before they become civilised. In *this* garden we plant a grown bougainvillaea, drape it over a wall that needs it, and can see it flowering densely and red the very next weekend, and the whole year round until its lack of self-control must be restrained. The garden is about twenty acres. It lies two kilometres from the coast and consists of the inner part of a peninsula which juts out like a hillock into a lagoon fringed with coconut trees. Ten years ago, when the owner, Mr. Geoffrey Bawa, bought the place, it consisted of a house with frosted-glass windows (matt glass in the windows), arches and the like, and the land was planted with old rubber trees. He was a lawyer then, but has since become an architect. The garden has grown without a plan, following a principle of "Action Gardening", named after "Action Painting" where the painter throws his colours at the canvas from a great distance.

The plants are a miracle. Those that flower do so the whole year round, and the leaves have all shapes, sizes and colours. There are long white leaves over two metres long and fat, fire-red leaves which the light shines through. There are beautiful ferns and formal plants whose regular leaves are arranged like a child's drawing. The Temple tree can be formed and twisted. In front of the house is a eight-year old Temple tree, which consists really of *two* trees whose stems were twisted round each other, after which the branches were weighed down with big stones so that they stand out almost horizontally and the leaves make a large flat parasol. When a family of peacocks settles on its branches it is like staring at a Chinese plate. At the foot of a system of stairs, where the garden has recently grown over half an acre of paddy fields, a grove of Temple trees was planted three months ago. On each branch hangs a long string with a large stone at the end of it as if one had stepped into a medieval description of a fantastic journey. In another place a six-metre-high Travellers' palm, which is so formal that it grows in one plane and only looks like a line from the side, has been pulled and dragged four times over an area of three acres until it was placed suitably.

The subsoil consists of a scarlet-coloured rock called *cabook*, which is so soft that you can cut it in blocks the size of a gas concrete block. In a discreet corner of the garden, two old men sit slicing *cabook* that is then placed into a steady stream of bullock-carts and fed to the new stairs and walls and buildings. The *cabook*-mines lie on the slope of the hill down to the lagoon; in 5 or 6 years they will stand as an immense system of terraces with lemon trees, a 100-metre-long ramp leading to the lagoon, stairs and walls cut out of the ground. Meanwhile the steady stream of stones puts a heavy pressure on your weekends, which is when all work is done, for if they are not used they are piled. A simple little staircase leading from a terrace down to a place that used to be a boathouse, (built five years ago but now already a ruin,) grew in a few months to an 'Egyptian'-scale construction.

The house itself grows with new rooms and garages and outdoor bathrooms of leaves as huge as yourself. Foundations have been abolished as they take too much time, cost too much in cement. That kind of building does not look old quickly enough and, what is worse, a wall with foundations cannot be pushed over if later it stands in the way of something better.

On both sides of the house is a deep vista through the garden and across the lagoon. In one direction you can see three kilometres away to a hillock rising from the lagoon with a Dagoba, a bell-shaped temple building. By placing a big old Portuguese jar under an old tree in the middle distance, several square kilometres of lagoon and jungle and even the temple itself have been drawn into the garden. It is strange how one can civilise a whole landscape with a single pot. In the other direction you see a steep little overgrown island. At night it stands in sharp silhouette every 13 seconds from a light-house six kilometres up the coast. The next project is to civilise the island with an equestrian statue on the top. The statue has already been found, a horseman in bronze from the Boer War. The local council has it replaced after Ceylon became independent. But nobody knows how to get it onto the island.

Three people work permanently. On arrival at the weekend, the first they do is to place a comfortable chair on the spot in the garden from which the work can best be directed. A silver-tray with tea and cheese toast, and then half the population of the nearest village, both men and women, are fetched. They come silently out among the leaves and begin to work. Twenty women can move a mountain in small baskets on their heads. Two men stamp the clay until it can be used as mortar; others lay the blocks. A tree which is in the way is moved to a neutral spot until it can be used later.

Recently, whilst finishing the stair and the hill was being cut steeply behind, ferns were being planted, wondering whether the fields should be lowered or rised, whether one should build a series of two-metre-high pyramids in the paddy fields below, it was suddenly realised that a view was hidden behind 150 metres of trees and plants. The comfortable chairs were turned around, the other work was stopped, and in a few hours trees were felled, undergrowth removed, branches cut, snakes killed, and a whole new view — and garden — was made.

Garden essay by Ulrik Plesner appeared in *Arkitekten* (Denmark), 1959. Republished courtesy of the author and *Arkitekten*.

HOUSES

ENA DE SILVA HOUSE, COLOMBO

THE ARCHITECT'S HOUSE, COLOMBO

STANLEY DE SARAM HOUSE, COLOMBO

PETER WHITE HOUSE, MAURITIUS

LIDIA GUNASEKERA HOUSE, BENTOTA

SUNETRA NANAYAKARA HOUSE, HORAGOLLA

PAVILIONS, BATUJIMBAR, BALI

ENA DE SILVA HOUSE, COLOMBO

This house was built for a friend, Ena de Silva, soon after Geoffrey Bawa started practice. There was close cooperation and understanding between client and architect throughout the design and building stages, with the certain knowledge that the house would be lived in well.

All the building materials were local — except for the very little glass that was used and the steel reinforcement for the first floor slab and supporting frame. The large mango tree in the courtyard was on the site, but the other almost-as-large Plumeria was brought in with the help of an elephant, a tractor, and a host of helpers. The ground floor paving is of granite, cut and also uncut, as in the courtyard; the walls are of brick and plaster, and the roof of tiles.

Batik mural in the patio of the house.

View through the living room from the patio.

DE SILVA HOUSE

Section.

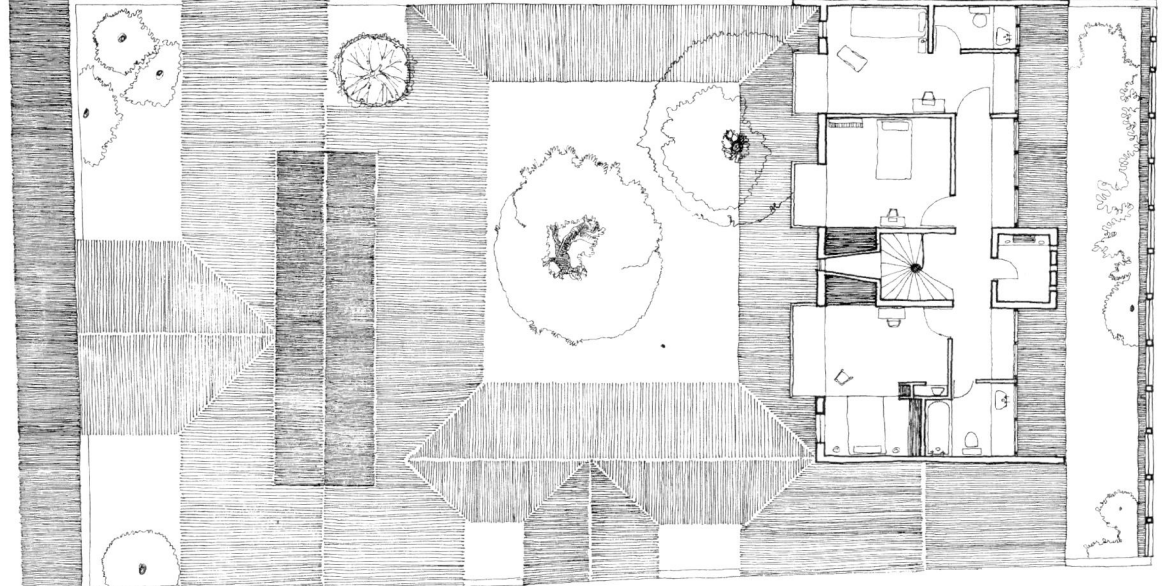

First floor plan.

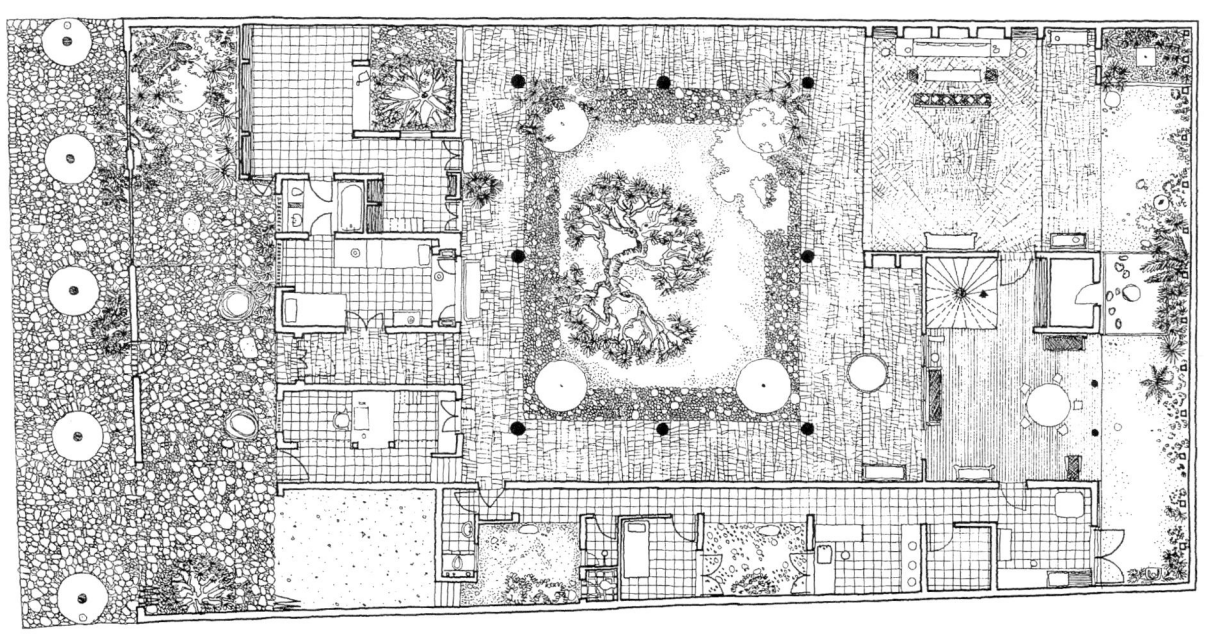

Ground floor plan.

View through the bedroom courtyard.

Bubble fountain.

DE SILVA HOUSE

View of the central patio through shuttered window.

View of roofs with central patio on the right.

THE ARCHITECT'S HOUSE, COLOMBO

Geoffrey Bawa moved into a quarter of the present house in 1958, when he leased and altered the second of four small houses in a bylane off of a bylane, off of Bagatelle Road in Colombo. The first house consisted, after it had been altered, of a living room, bedroom, diminutive kitchen, and a servant's room and bathroom, and it was the third house down the lane. The fourth house then became vacant and so a dining room and second living room were added. In 1968 the first and second houses were bought and the lane became redundant, so all four houses and the lane now constitute the present house. The first of the houses was demolished and a new structure built to contain a library on the first floor, and gardens on the second and third levels.

Main entrance to the house.

View from the garage down the entrance hallway.

Second floor plan.

First floor plan.

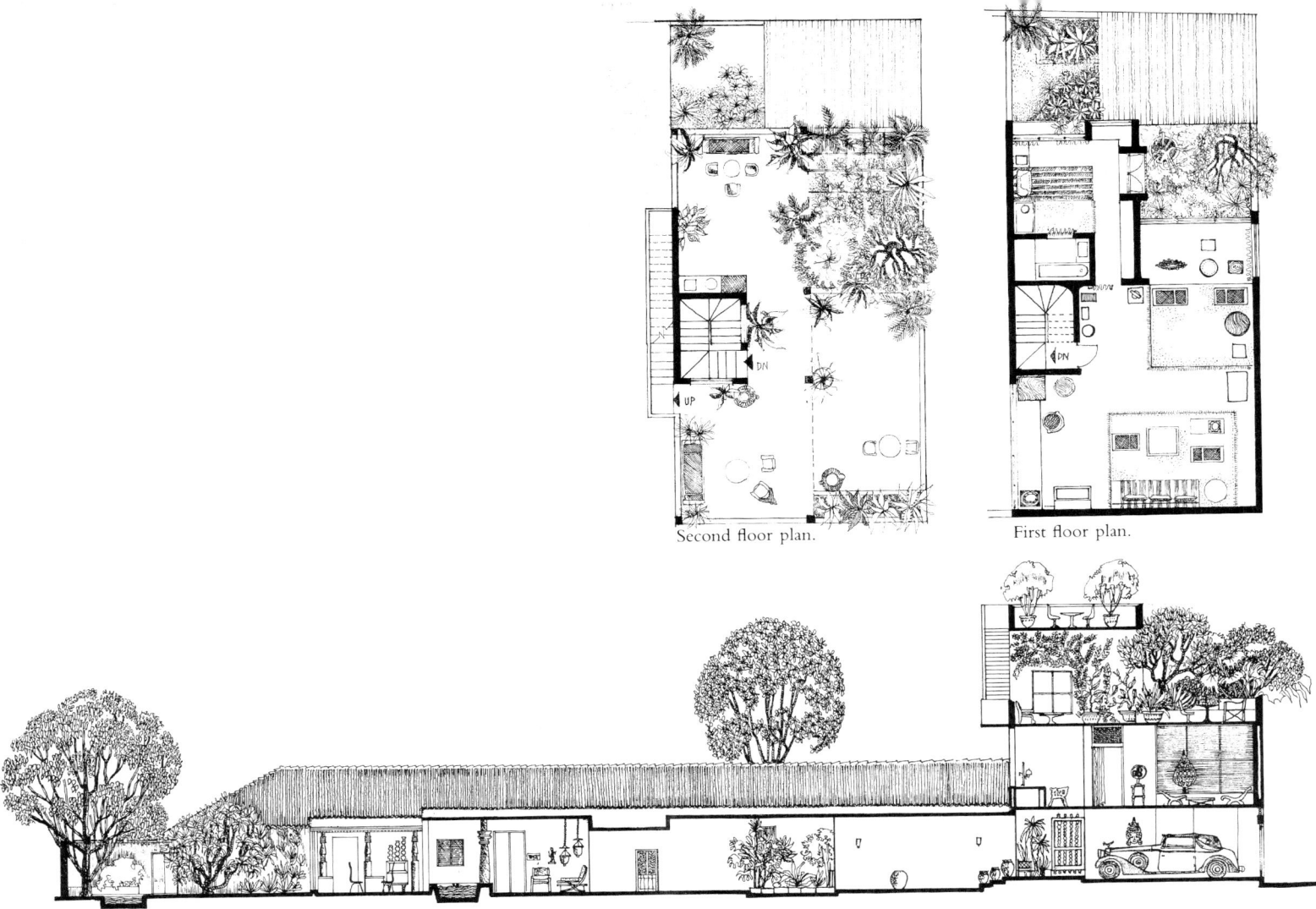

Longitudinal section.

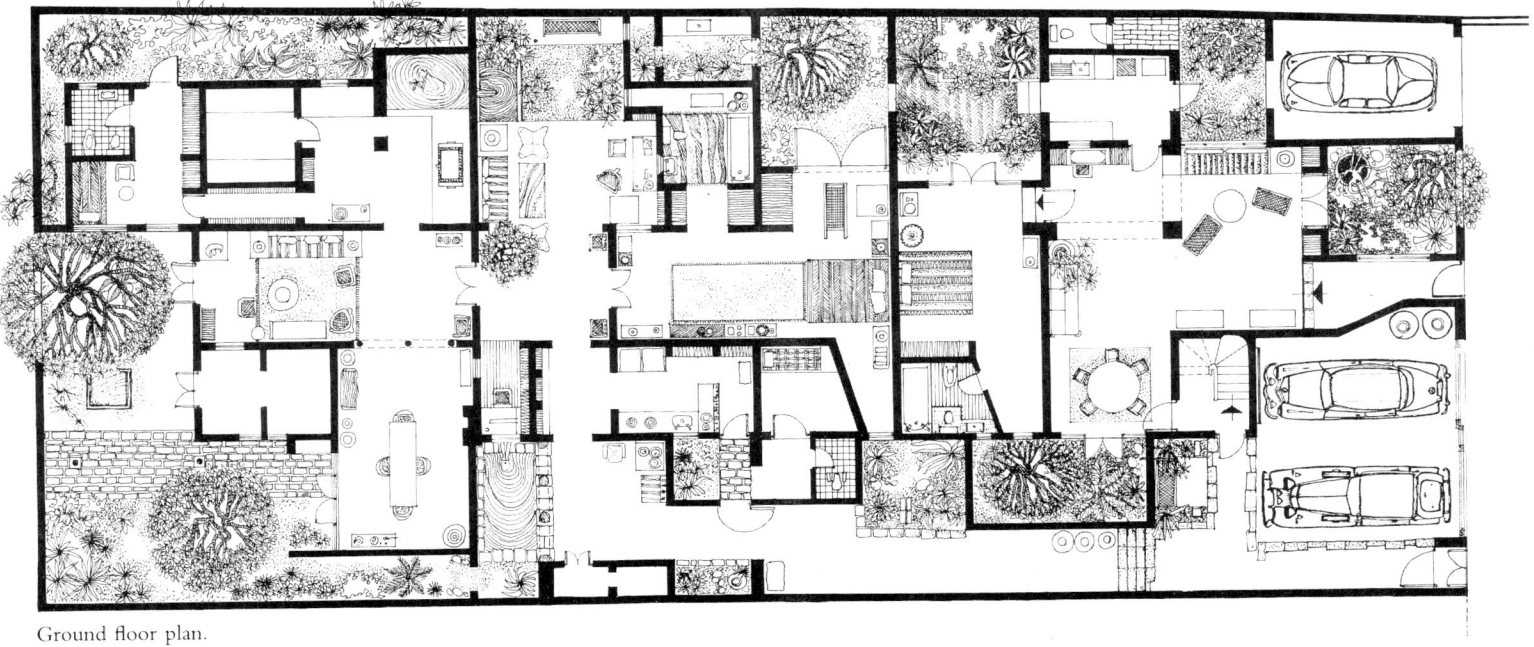

Ground floor plan.

51

Patio with bench adjacent to central sitting room.

Columns at end of entrance hallway.
Door painted by D. Friend.

View from bedroom towards the rear garden.

Room for reflection on ground floor at rear.

Dining room.

Decorated door to upstairs sitting room. Stairs to roof terrace.

ARCHITECT'S HOUSE

Upstairs sitting room.

Roof terrace.

STANLEY DE SARAM HOUSE, COLOMBO

This house was built on the front lawn of the large house which the de Sarams had long lived in. They had a collection of bought and inherited antiques, mainly sixteenth and seventeenth century, and the de Sarams being old friends, the design was almost 'talked' into its final form, so that these various antiques would sit well and be most aptly placed.

Moving from a house well set back from the roadway to a site right up against the pavement made both security and privacy prime considerations, and the interior courtyards had to be as large as possible to compensate for the loss of a garden.

Entrance gate.

Inner courtyard.

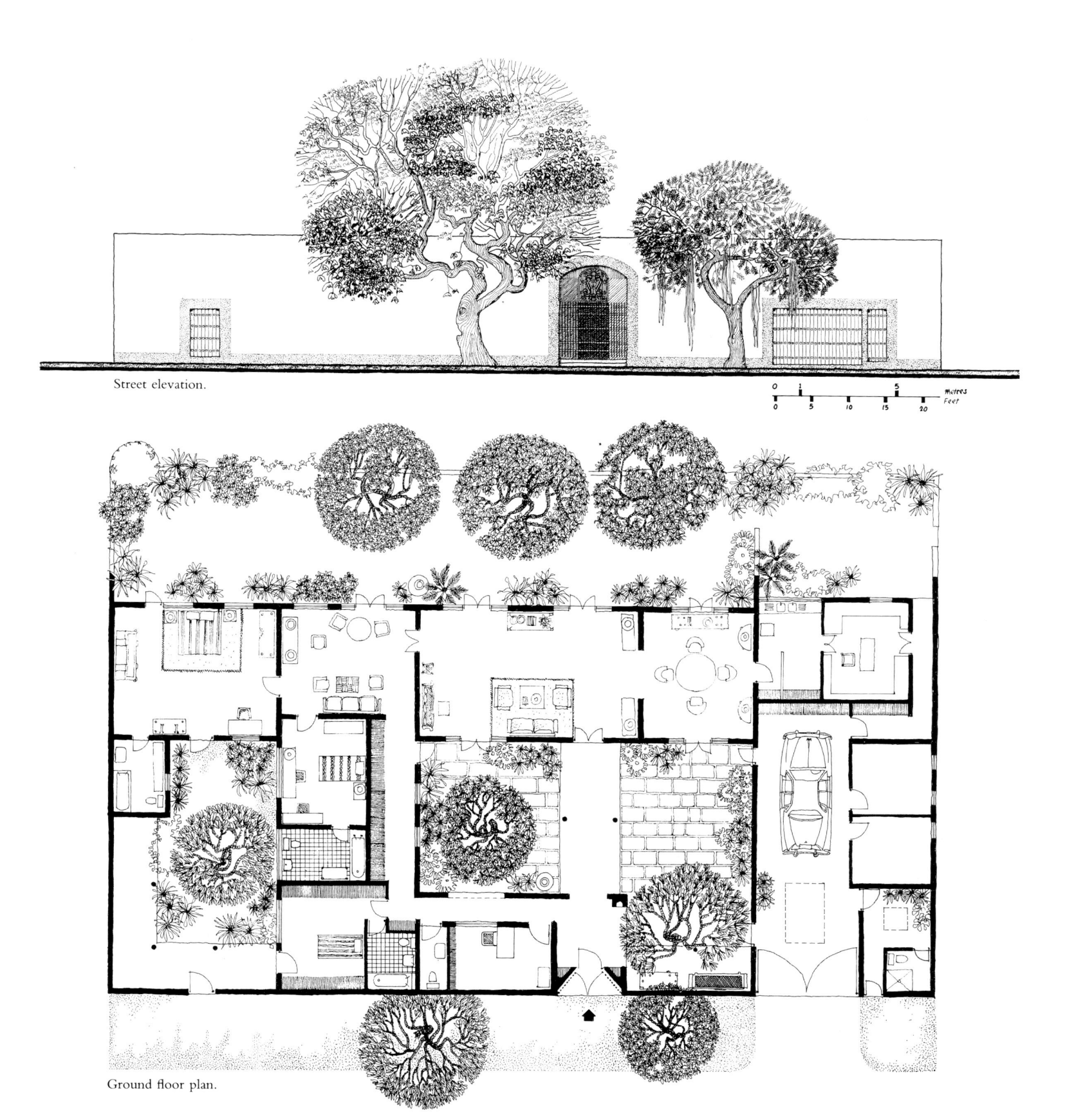

DE SARAM HOUSE

Street elevation.

Ground floor plan.

PETER WHITE HOUSE, MAURITIUS

Peter White, the owner, bought the partially ruined but beautifully proportioned old sugar cane warehouses to restore and use as a weekend country house, where he could relax in solitude or give an occasional large party. He had known Geoffrey Bawa in Colombo, and he invited him to visit Mauritius and to do virtually whatever he wanted to answer this simply stated need. There is a bedroom, a bathroom, and a small kitchen. The remaining space is left free to be used as will and mood dictate. The remaining outbuildings contain three more bedrooms for guests.

Exterior view of east facade.

Lateral facade with fire escape.

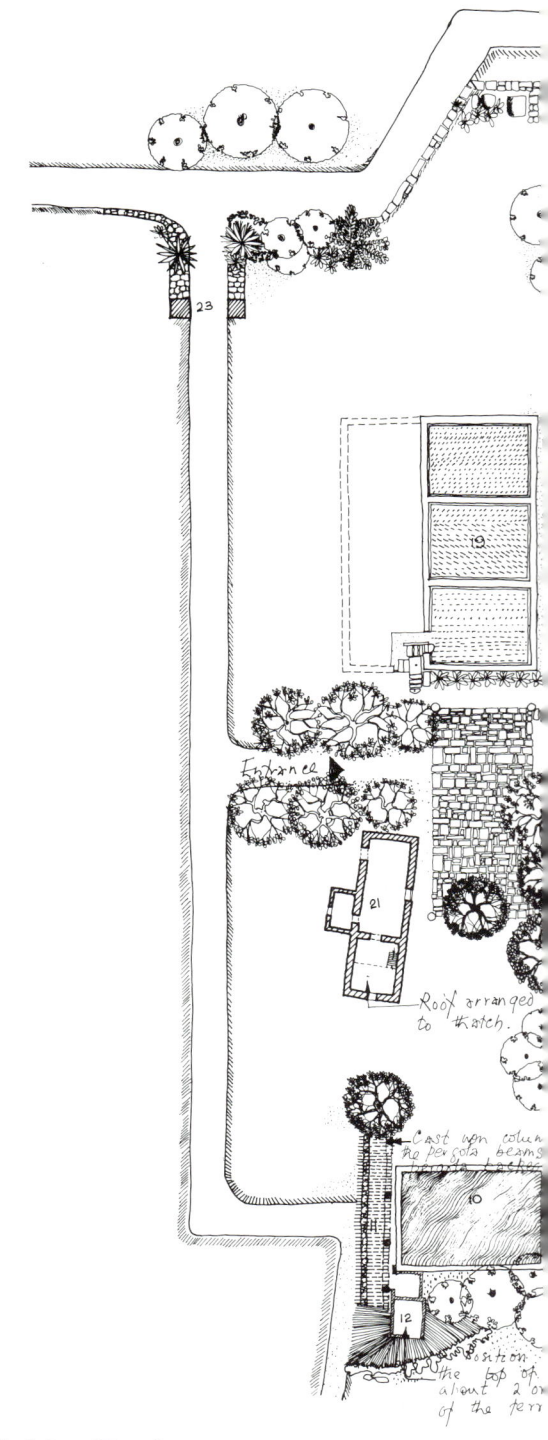

Le Vieux Moulin
a Pereybère.
Isle de Maurice.

Site plan annotated by the architect.

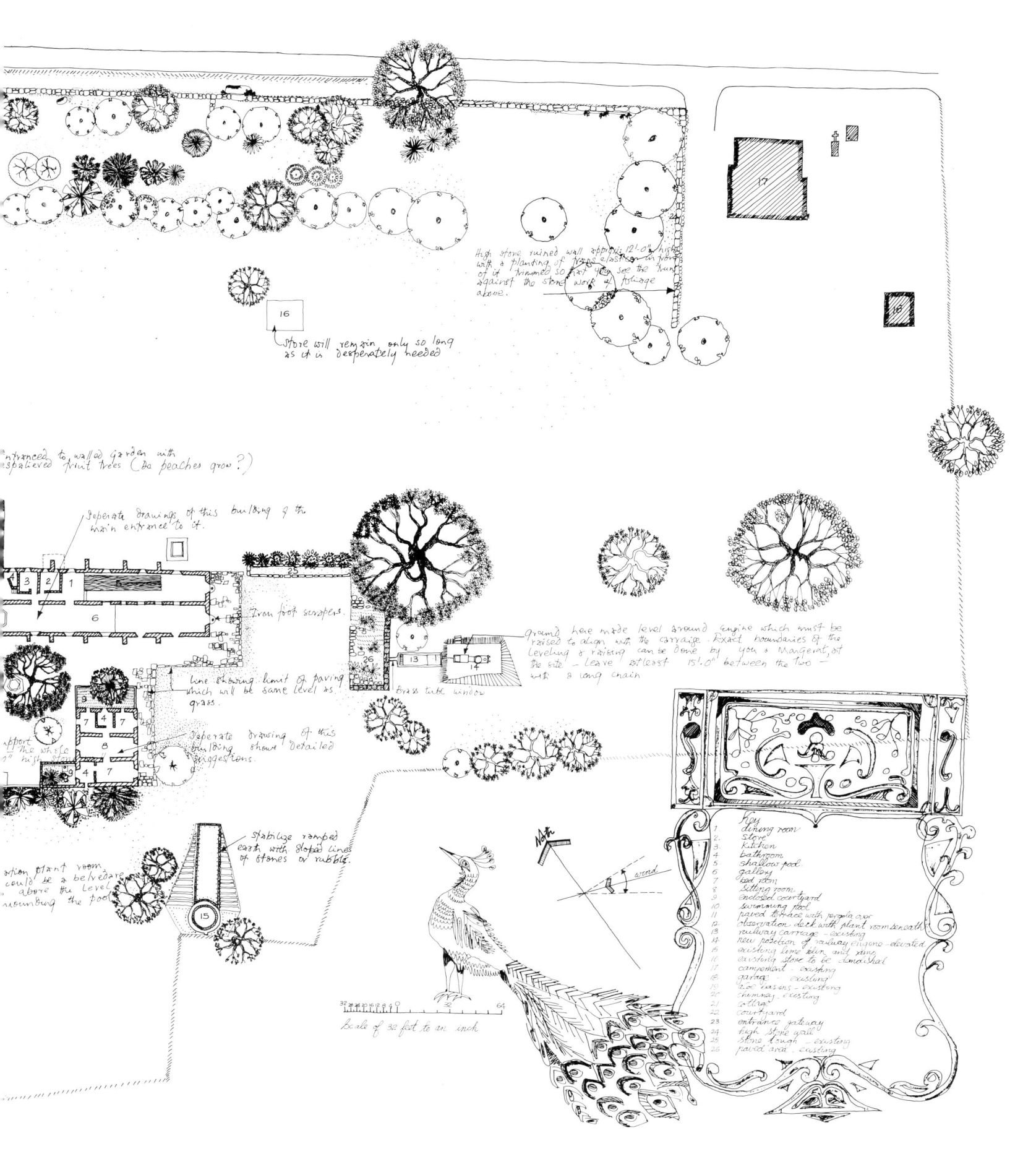

High stone ruined wall approx 12'-0" high with a planting of trees closer in front of it trimmed so that you see the trunk against the stone work & foliage above.

Store will remain only so long as it is desperately needed

Entrance to walled garden with espaliered fruit trees (Do peaches grow?)

Separate drawings of this building & the main entrance to it.

Iron foot scrapers.

Line showing limit of paving which will be same level as grass.

Brass tube window

Ground here made level around engine which must be raised to align with the carriage. Exact boundaries of the leveling & raising can be done by you & Margaret at the site — leave at least 15'-0" between the two — with a long chain

Separate drawing of this building shows detailed suggestions.

support the whole " high sla

tion plant room could be a belvedere above the level rounding the pool

Stabilize ramped earth with sloped lines of stones or rubble.

North
wind

Scale of 32 feet to an inch

Key
1. dining room
2. store
3. kitchen
4. bathroom
5. shallow pool
6. gallery
7. bed room
8. sitting room
9. enclosed courtyard
10. swimming pool
11. paved terrace with pergola over
12. observation deck with plant room beneath
13. railway carriage - existing
14. new position of railway engine - elevated
15. existing lime kiln and ring
16. existing stone to be demolished
17. campement - existing
18. garage - existing
19. aloe basins - existing
20. chimney - existing
21. cottage
22. courtyard
23. entrance gateway
24. high stone wall
25. stone trough - existing
26. paved area - existing

Vaulted dining room with pool.

View across vaulted room through open arched central wall.

Transversal sections of the vaulted spaces.

Bedroom.

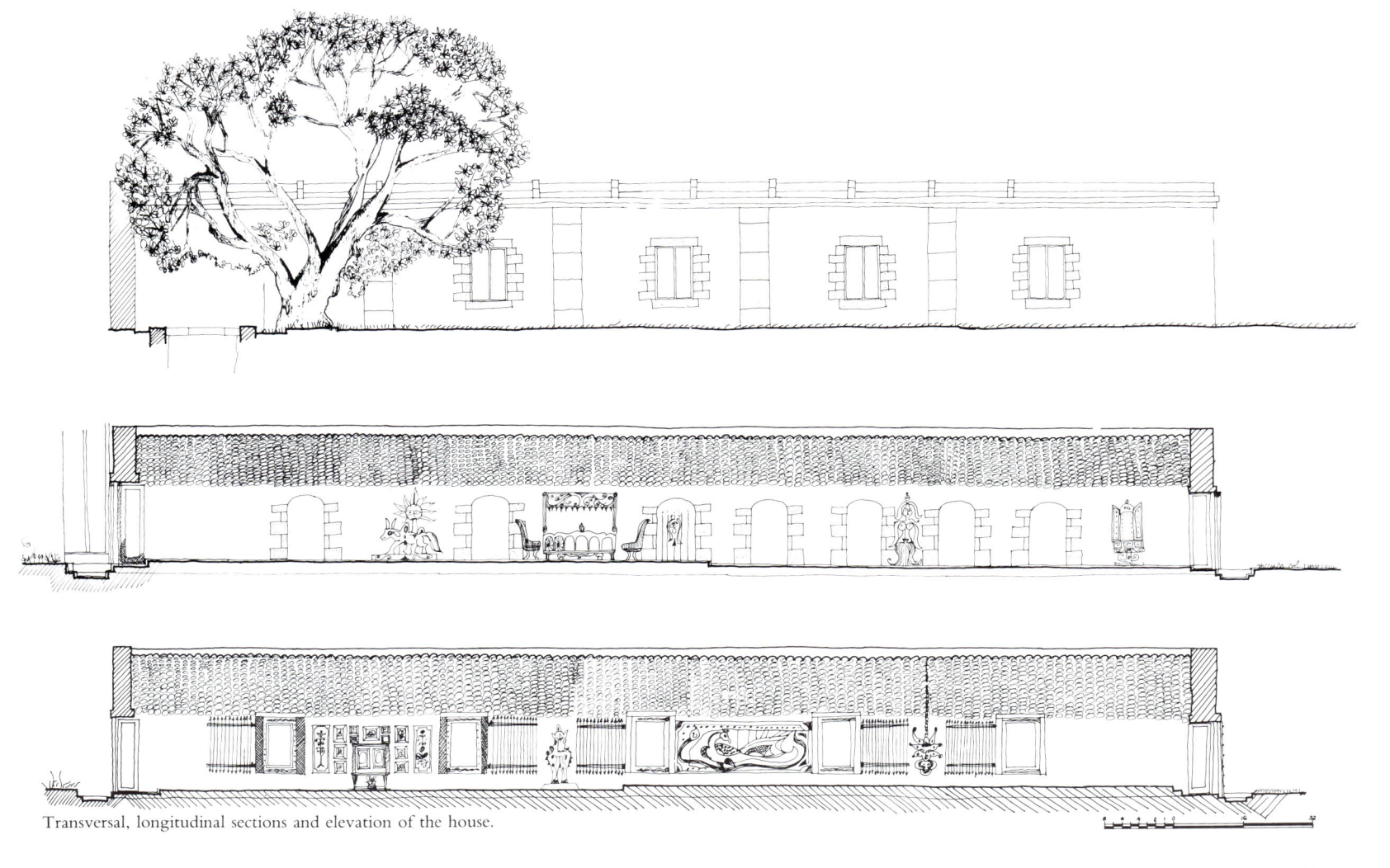

Transversal, longitudinal sections and elevation of the house.

HOUSES

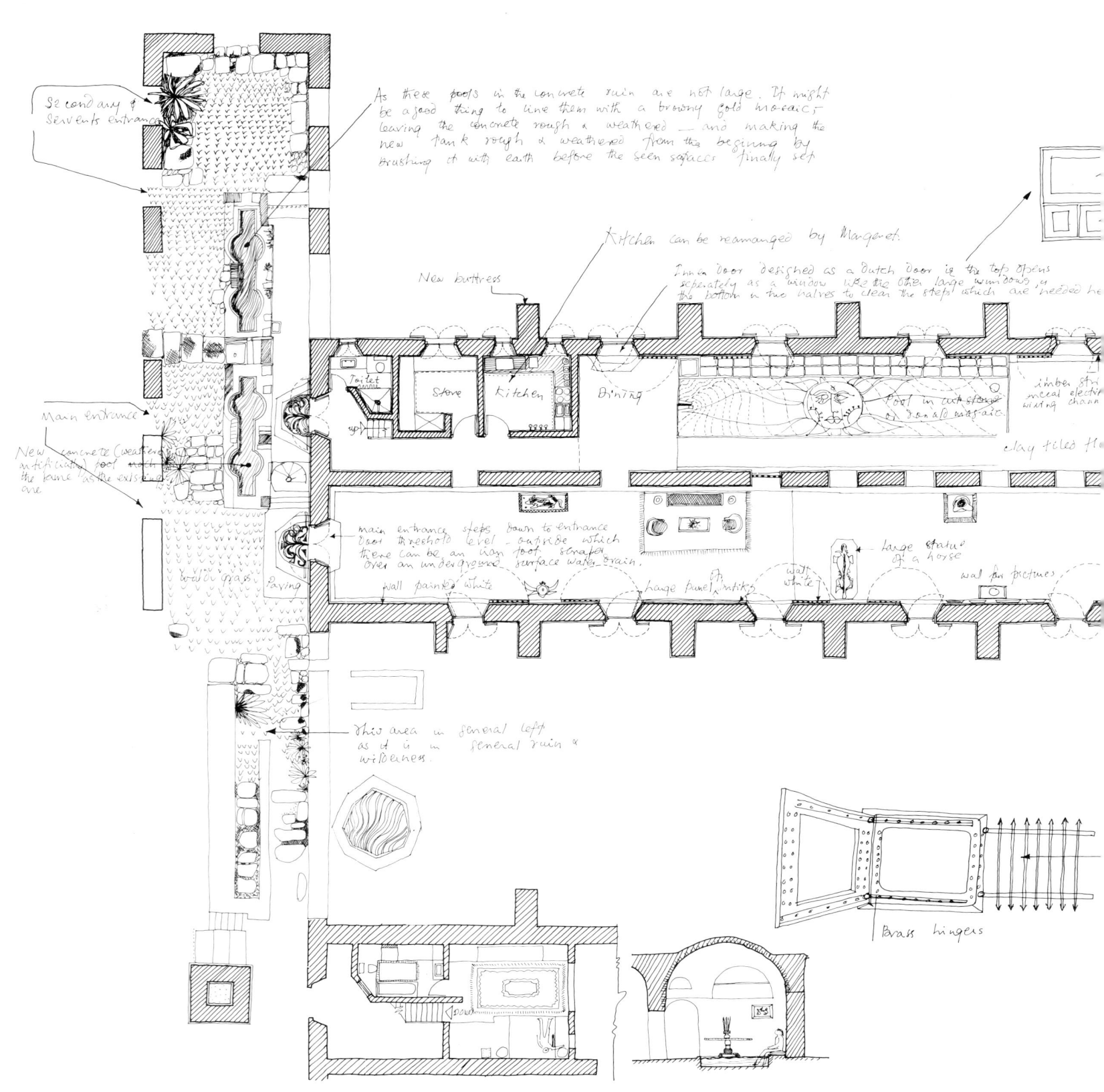

Annotated plans of the ground floor and mezzanine bedroom, section through dining area with pool.

64

WHITE HOUSE

s opens seperately

m sashes open after top sash opens

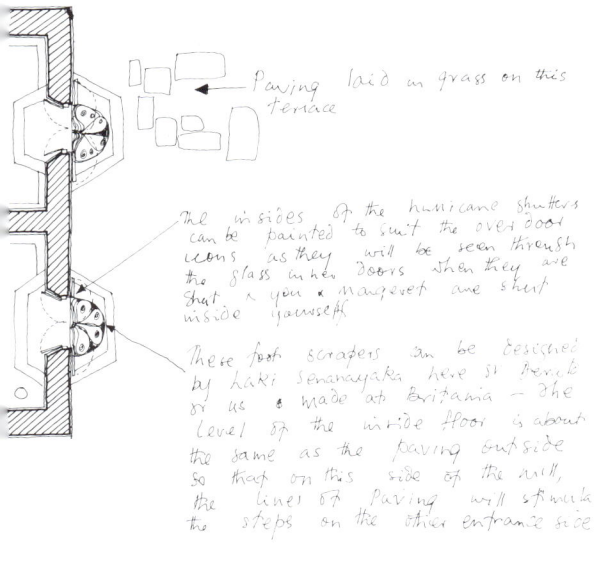

Paving laid in grass on this terrace

The insides of the hurricane shutters can be painted to suit the over door icons as they will be seen through the glass when doors when they are shut & you & marvoret are shut inside yourselfs

These foot scrapers can be designed by Laki Senanayake here st Kerub or us & made at Britania — The level of the inside floor is about the same as the paving outside so that on this side of the wall, the lines of paving will fit with the steps on the other entrance side

s wai grill won't look as heavy as its
en drawn. Nor will the window sash have
obs — only the hinge, but its drawn on here
you to get me a rough pricing to see
eather they canbe done or not.

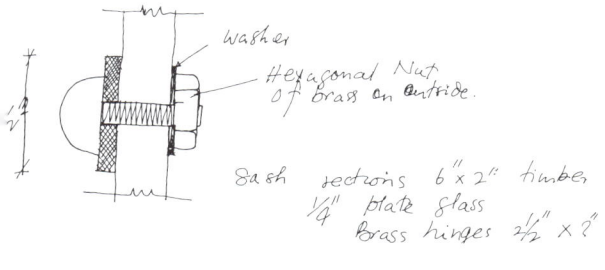

washer
Hexagonal Nut of brass on outside.

Sash sections 6"x 2" timber
¼" plate glass
Brass hinges 2½" x ?"

Ground floor interior view at night.

Living room.

LIDIA GUNASEKERA HOUSE, BENTOTA

The two houses on this site were originally built in 1720 and 1740. One of them was on the present site, the other on the other side of the road, and both were in a delapidated and miserable state, facing immediately onto the main Colombo-Galle road in Bentota. The site, approximately five acres, had magnificent trees and sloped from the high point of the main road back to ricefields on the eastern boundary.

The first house was turned back to front, walls were removed, the position of doorways changed, a verandah added to the east, and a blind wall built right along the full length of the property as presented to the roadway. The other house opposite was demolished with care, and as the walls were built of random stonework set in lime mortar, it was not difficult to remove the beautifully framed doorways and windows and upper floor wooden columns without damage. Exact measured drawings had been made of both houses, and when this house was rebuilt in its present position the changes made were chiefly the relocation of interior doorways and the addition of a staircase to reach the upper floor, which previously had been used only for storage and could only be reached by a steep insecure ladder. The other major change was to replace the entire walls to the front and back verandahs with large sheet glass where the walls had been, thus isolating the door and windows as beautiful objects set in glass, but being used as they always had been. It represents a marvellous exercise in adaptive reuse of traditional spaces.

View from the new house across the garden.

East facade of the old house.

View of the compound interior from verandah.

HOUSES

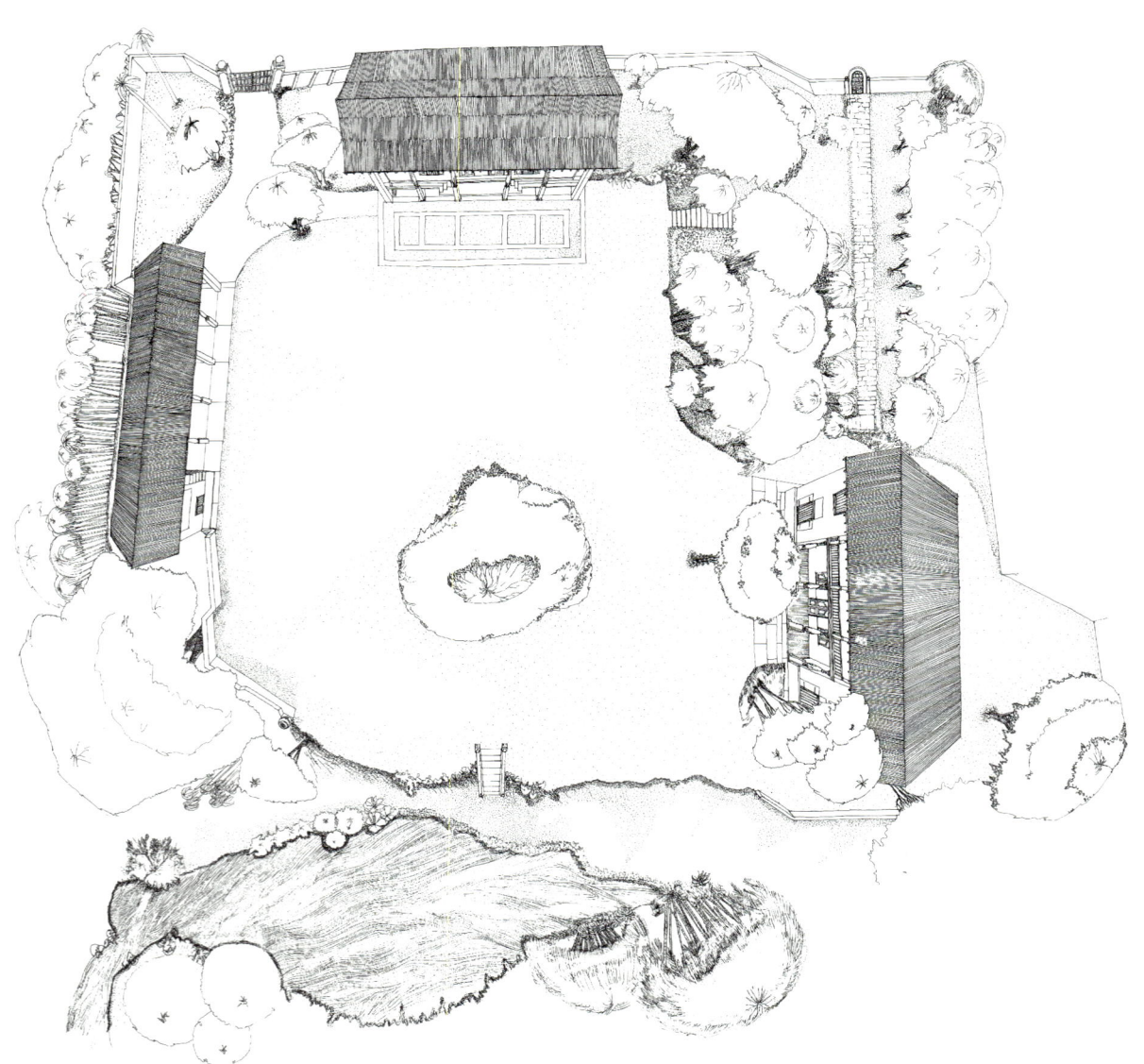

Porch of the new house.

Verandah and upper gallery.

Bird's-eye view of the grouped houses.

GUNASEKERA HOUSE

Ground floor plan and sections of the houses.

69

SUNETRA NANAYAKARA HOUSE, HORAGOLLA

The stables of the manor house or 'walauwa' were the starting point of the design of this house.

The stables were grand in scale and beautifully built and set the mood for the alterations and extensions that were needed. Being on an estate, there were no limitations of space so that whatever was added could have the same generosity of scale.

Elevation.

NANAYAKARA HOUSE

Section.

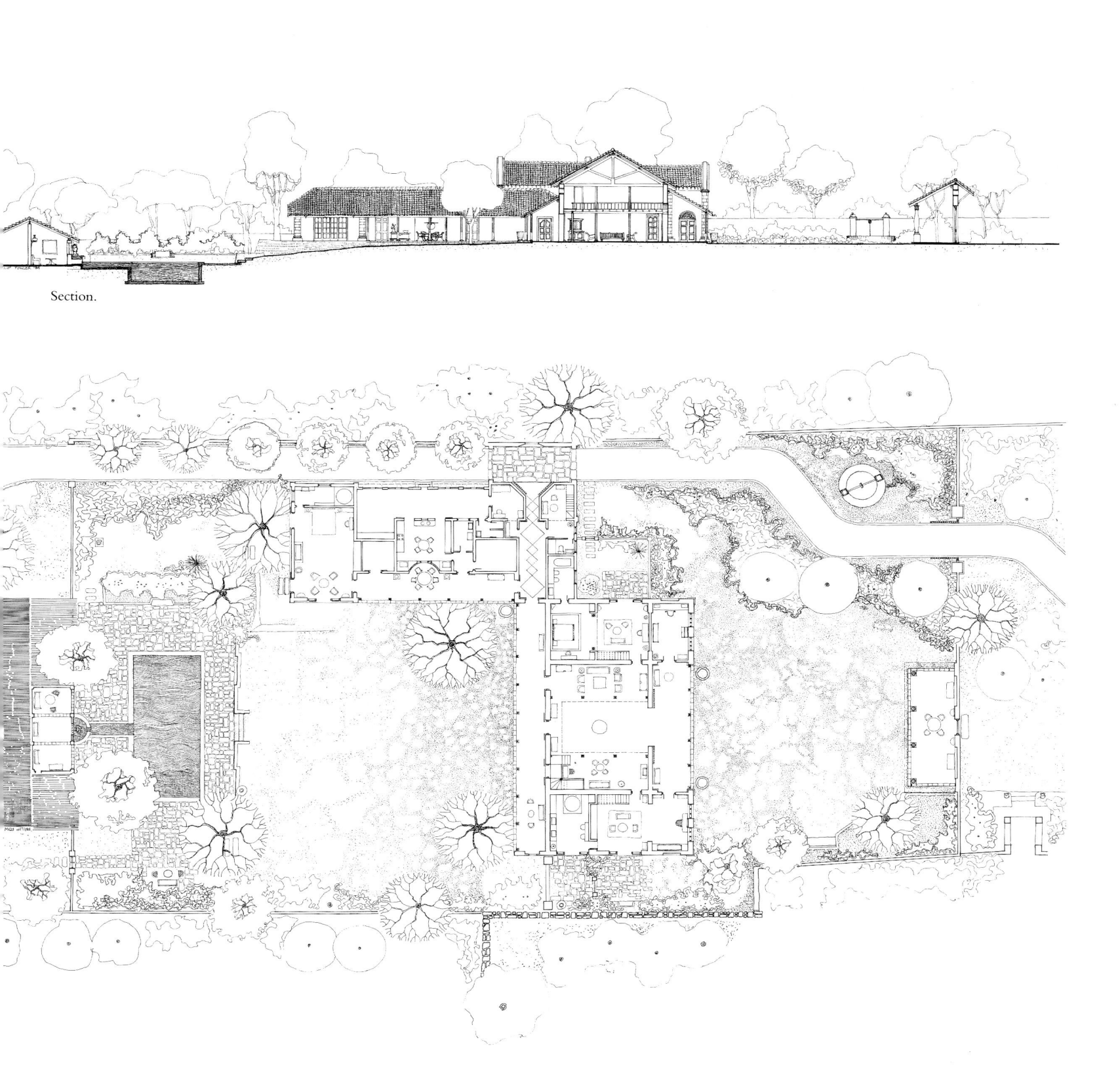

Ground floor plan with garden.

PAVILIONS, BATUJIMBAR, BALI

A project planned for Donald Friend the painter who, living in Bali, had bought land surrounding his house there, and wished to build a museum to display his splendid collection of bronzes and other *objets d'art*. Twelve houses were also planned, each separate and individual, to make up a complex of landscaped pavilions. Each house faced the beach and had approximately an acre of land; built into each were superb antique painted doors and columns. Constructed entirely in the Balinese local idiom, the builders, artisans, Donald Friend and Geoffrey Bawa participated in a marvellous collective enterprise.

Drawing of antique Balinese statue.

Staircase to the museum.

PAVILIONS

View from the dining pavilion verandah.

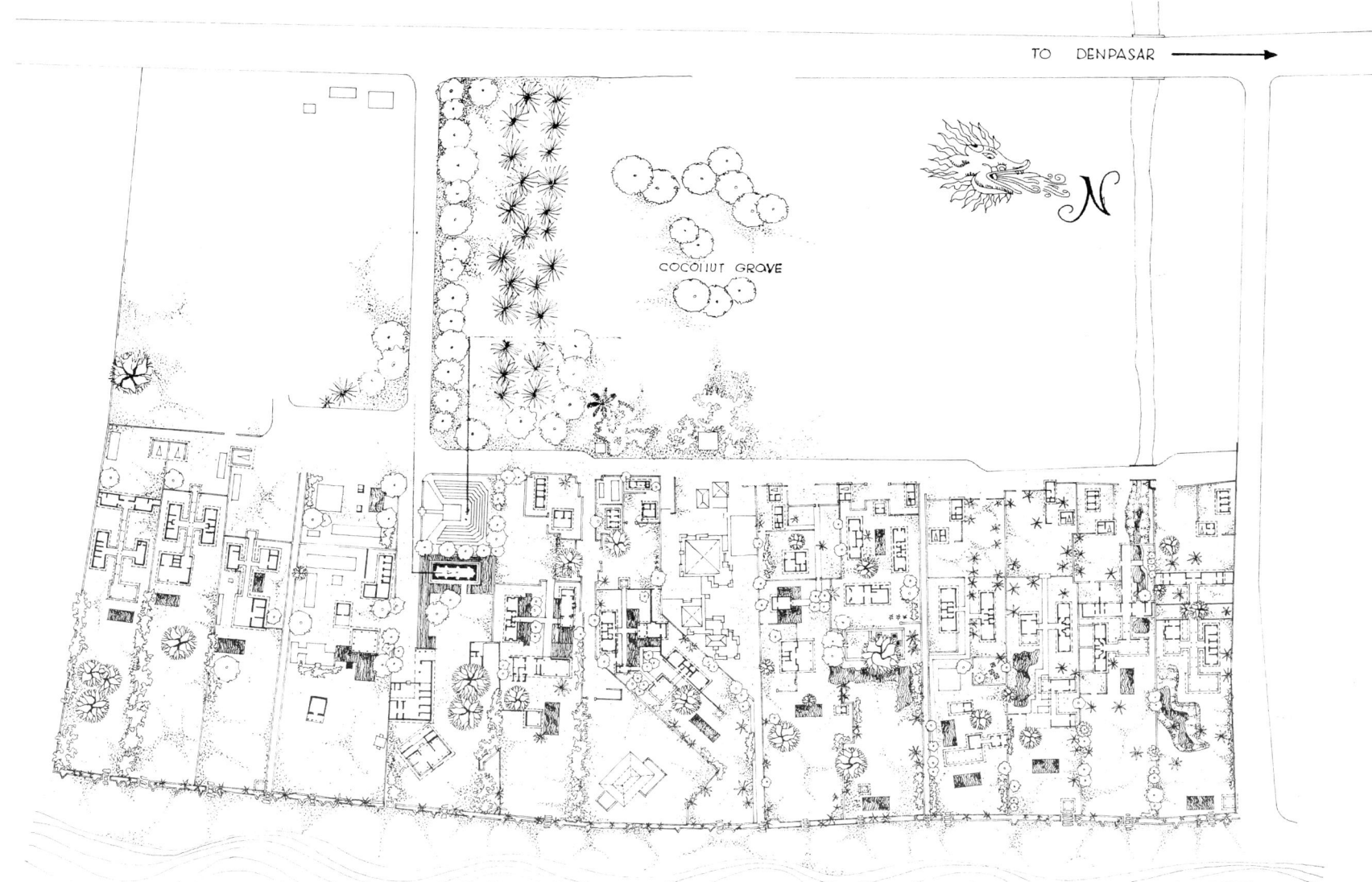

Plan of the lots and houses 1 to 15.

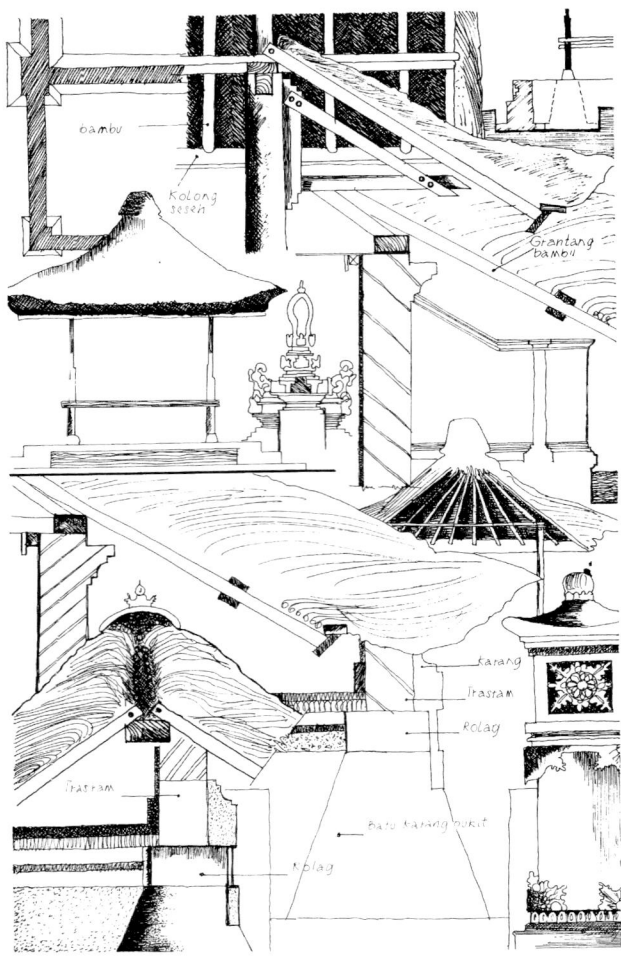

Series of detailed sketches of traditional Balinese building techniques.

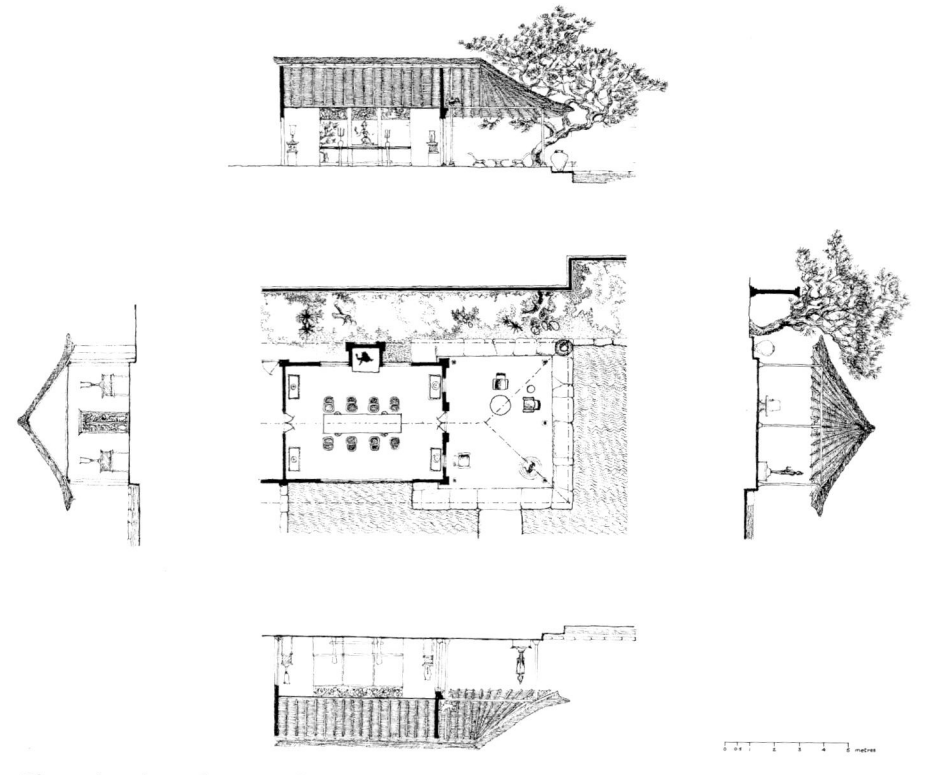

Plan and sections of House 6 dining pavilion.

Plan and sections of living pavilion and terrace, House 6.

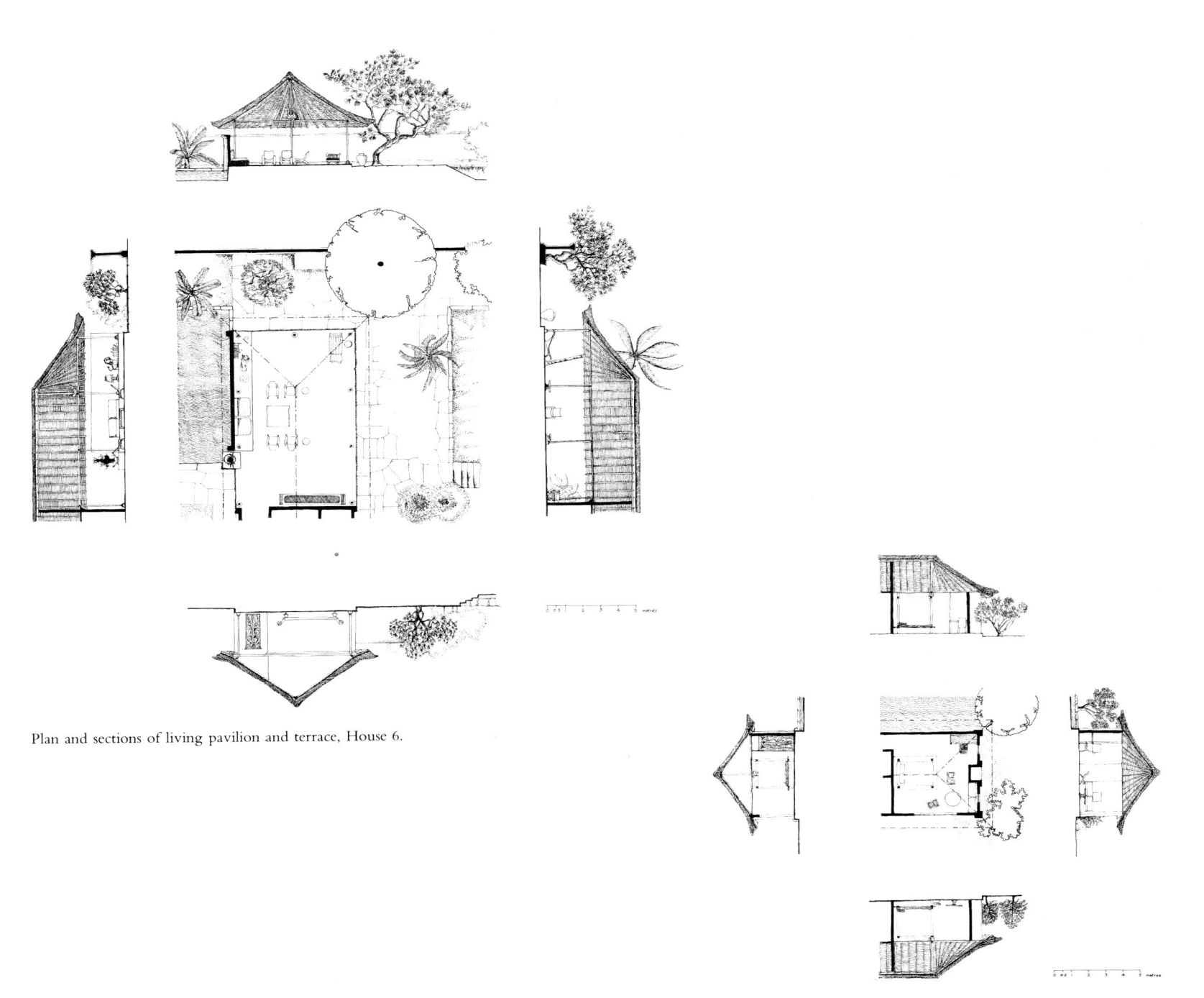

Plan and sections of bedroom in House 6.

HOUSES

Site and ground floor plan and section of House 6.

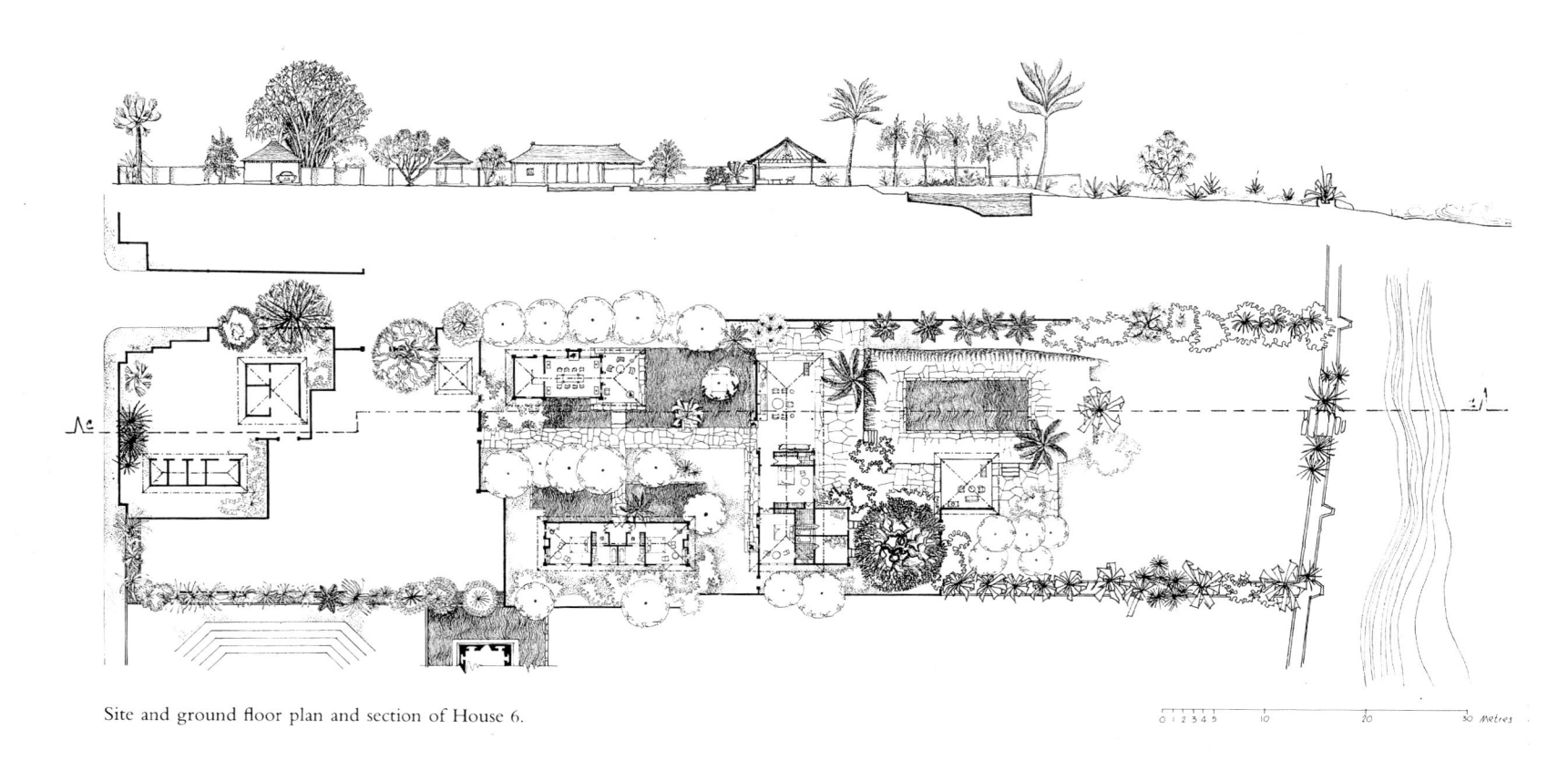

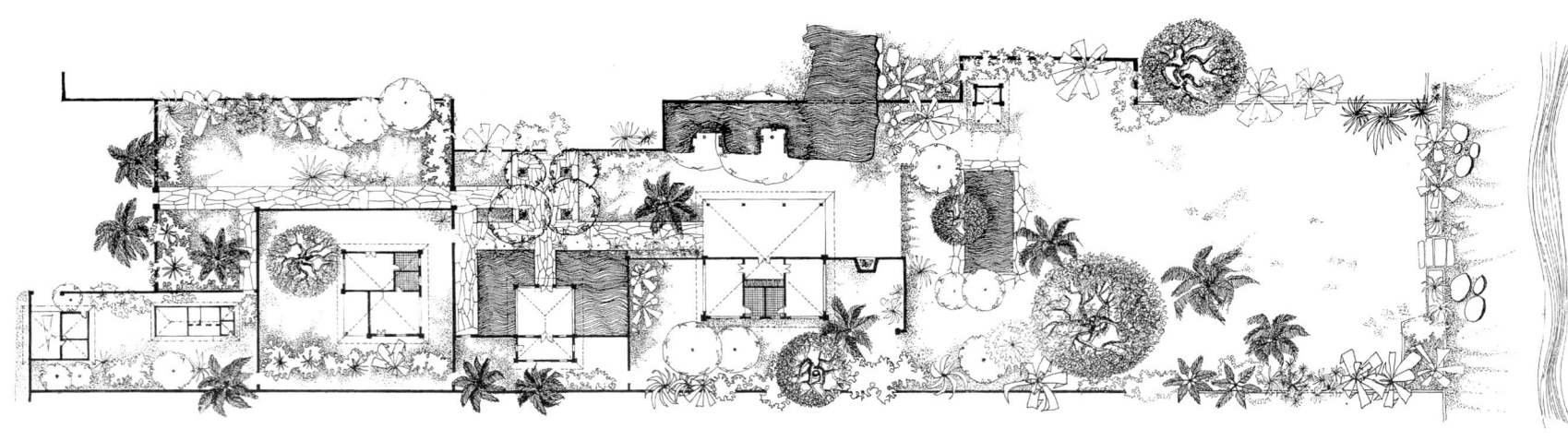

Site and ground floor plan of House 10.

Site and ground floor plan of House 15.

Site and ground floor plan of House 12.

HOUSES

Site and ground floor plan and section of House 11.

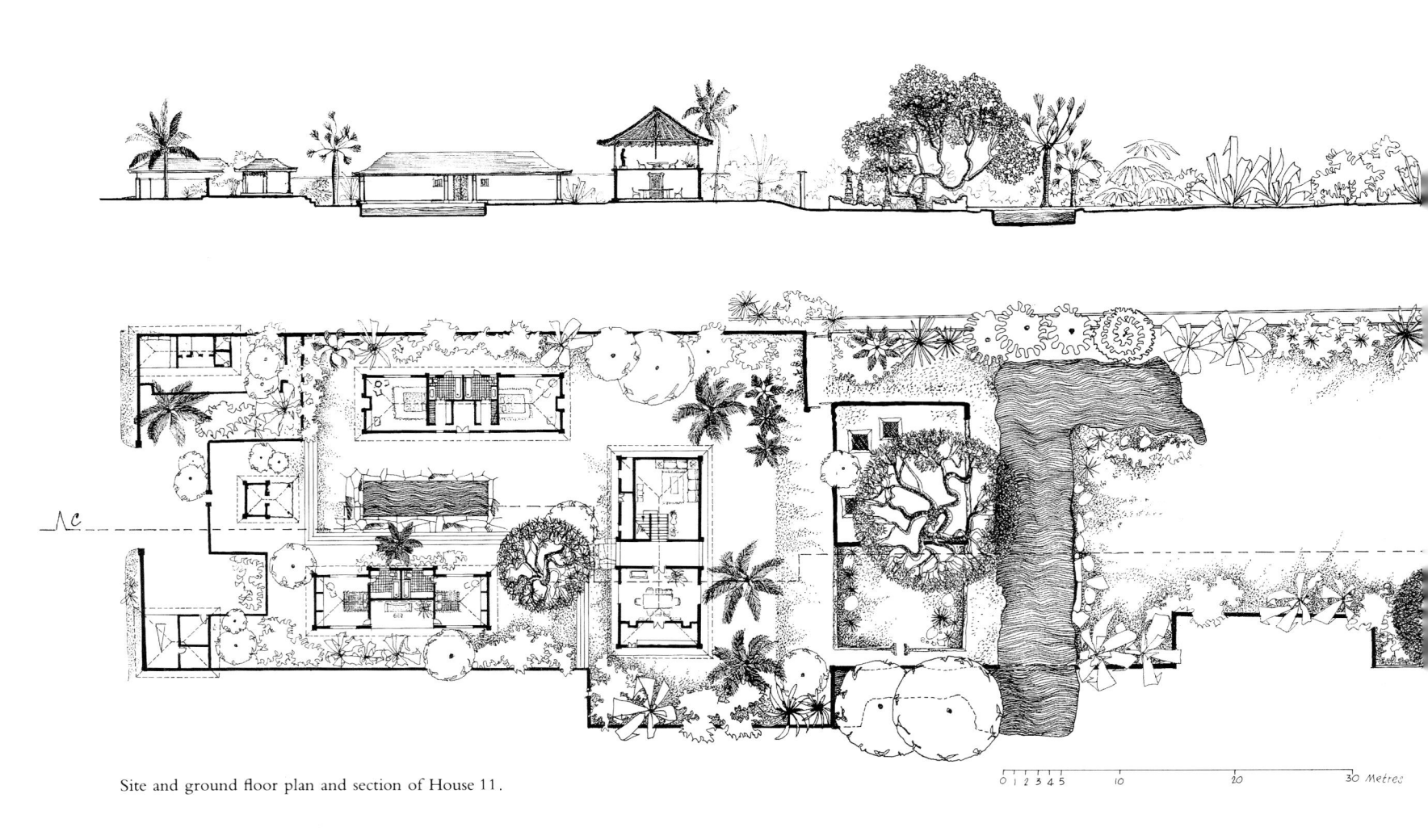

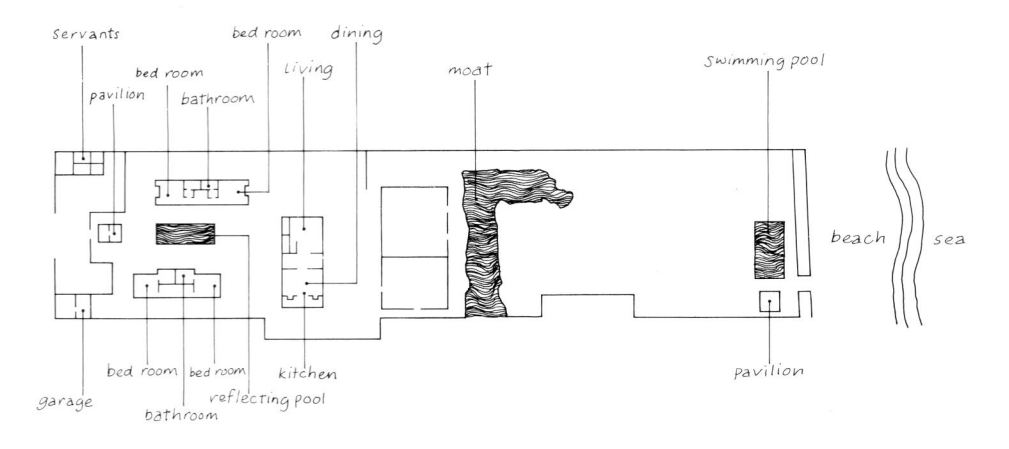

Key to organisation of the site.

Labels: servants, pavilion, bed room, bed room, bathroom, living, dining, moat, swimming pool, beach, sea, garage, bed room, bed room, bathroom, kitchen, reflecting pool, pavilion

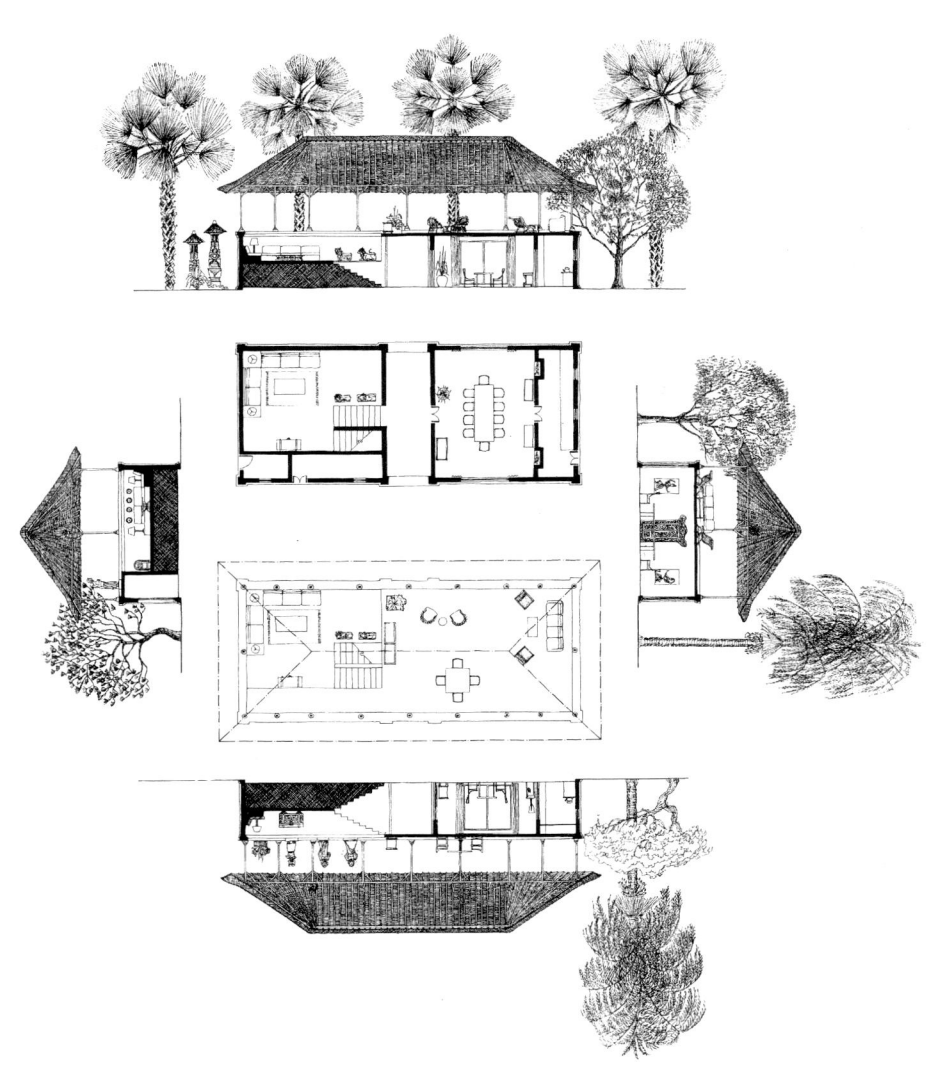

Ground and upper floor plan and sections of living and dining pavilions.

HOUSES

House with reflecting pool.

SCHOOLS

ST. BRIDGET'S MONTESSORI SCHOOL,
COLOMBO

YAHAPATH ENDERA FARM SCHOOL,
HANWELLA

INTEGRAL EDUCATION CENTRE,
PILIYANDALA

UNIVERSITY OF RUHUNU, MATARA
ARTS AND SCIENCE FACULTIES

ST. BRIDGET'S MONTESSORI SCHOOL, COLOMBO

This extremely low cost school is for very young children. The aim was for the children to feel as free as possible, and to create a world which they could identify with as their own. The "child world" of classroom and verandah goes up to 3 feet — cupboard and balustrade height — and above this the building is entirely open. The structure can be visually understood by any intelligent four-year-old, and the first floor slab and wide roof give the needed sense of shelter — from both sun and rain. The impression is that of being under a wide and splendid tree.

Facade corner detail.

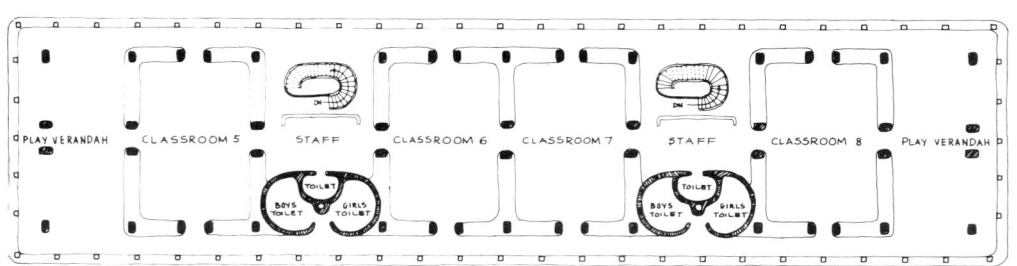

Elevation.

Section.

First floor plan.

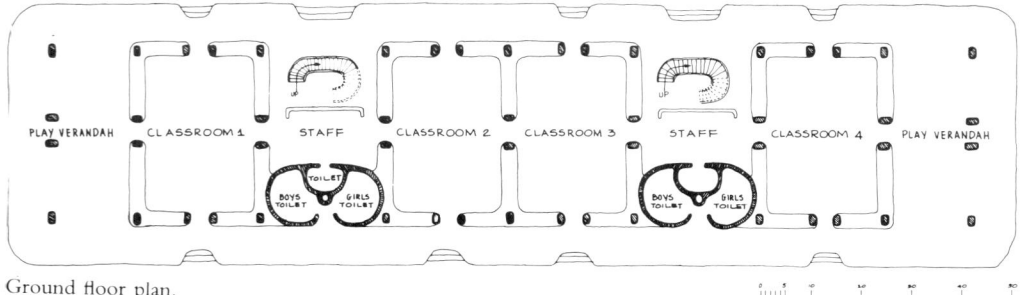

Ground floor plan.

Staircase.

YAHAPATH ENDERA FARM SCHOOL, HANWELLA

Hanwella School was the brainchild of Mother Good Counsel of the Good Shepherd Congregation, who wanted to start an educational centre for training orphan girls in order to give them a sound technical base in all aspects of farming and agriculture. Planned to house sixty girls at a time, and twelve nuns who were themselves well trained, it was to be a small self-sufficient community which would produce persons of confidence and knowledge who would contribute to the well-being and progress of the villages where they would eventually live.

The nucleus of the complex was the existing small house in which the previous manager of the estate (coconut and rubber) had lived. This was altered on the first site visit to accommodate the five pioneer nuns and a few girls. Subsequently it became the convent, and next came the farm buildings, the main centre, the girls' dormitories, kitchens, living space, etc. These were, with a little changing of the contours of the ridge on which the school was built, given splendid views from all buildings.

It was important to end up with a building that related to buildings in the countryside with which the girls were familiar, and this was achieved and formed the visual framework within which this particular education, technical, practical and spiritual, could blossom.

View of the complex from a distance.

FARM SCHOOL

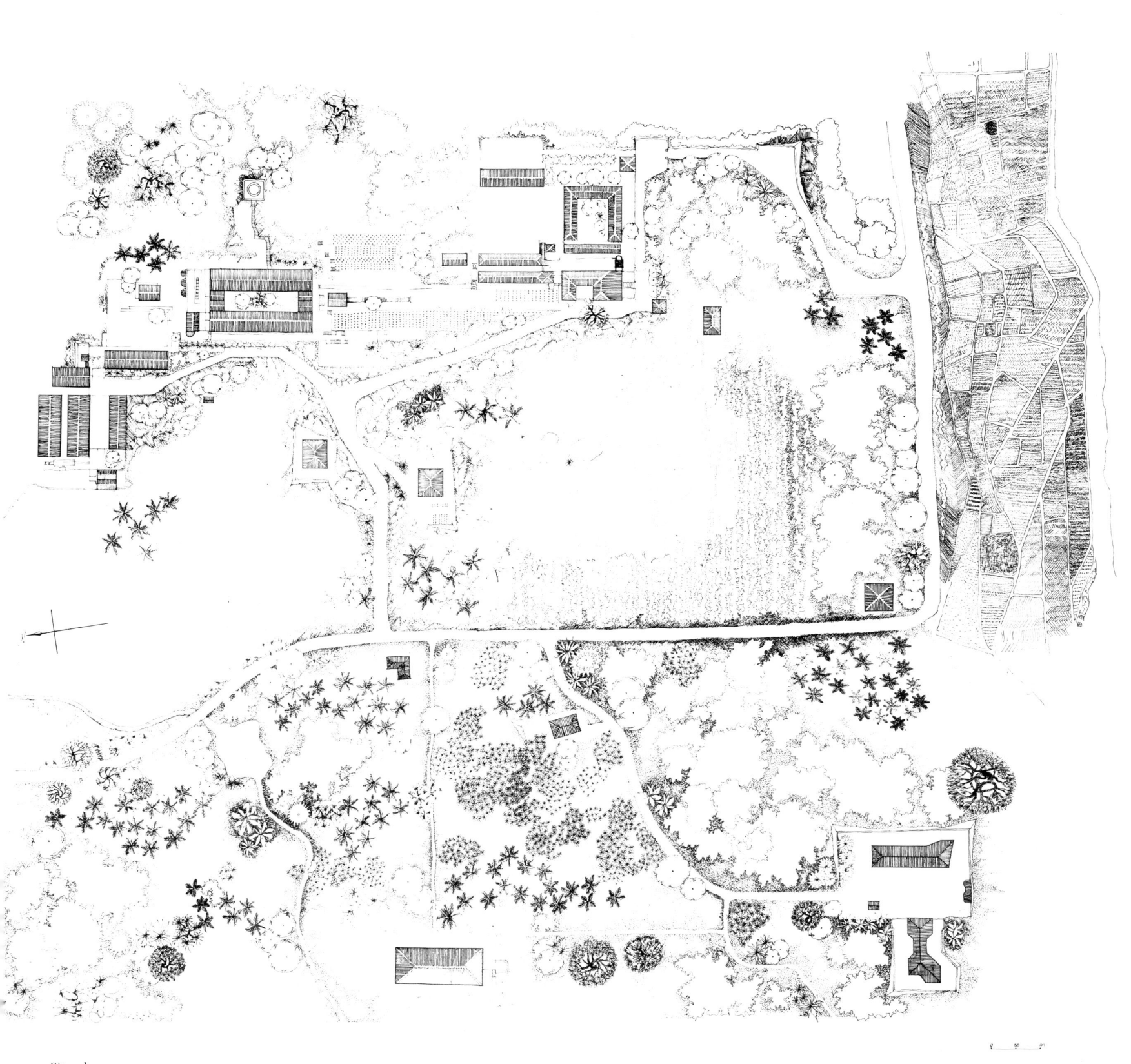

Site plan.

85

SCHOOLS

Elevation of the school buildings.

Entrance ramp.

Priest's house.

FARM SCHOOL

Chickenhouse (foreground).

87

SCHOOLS

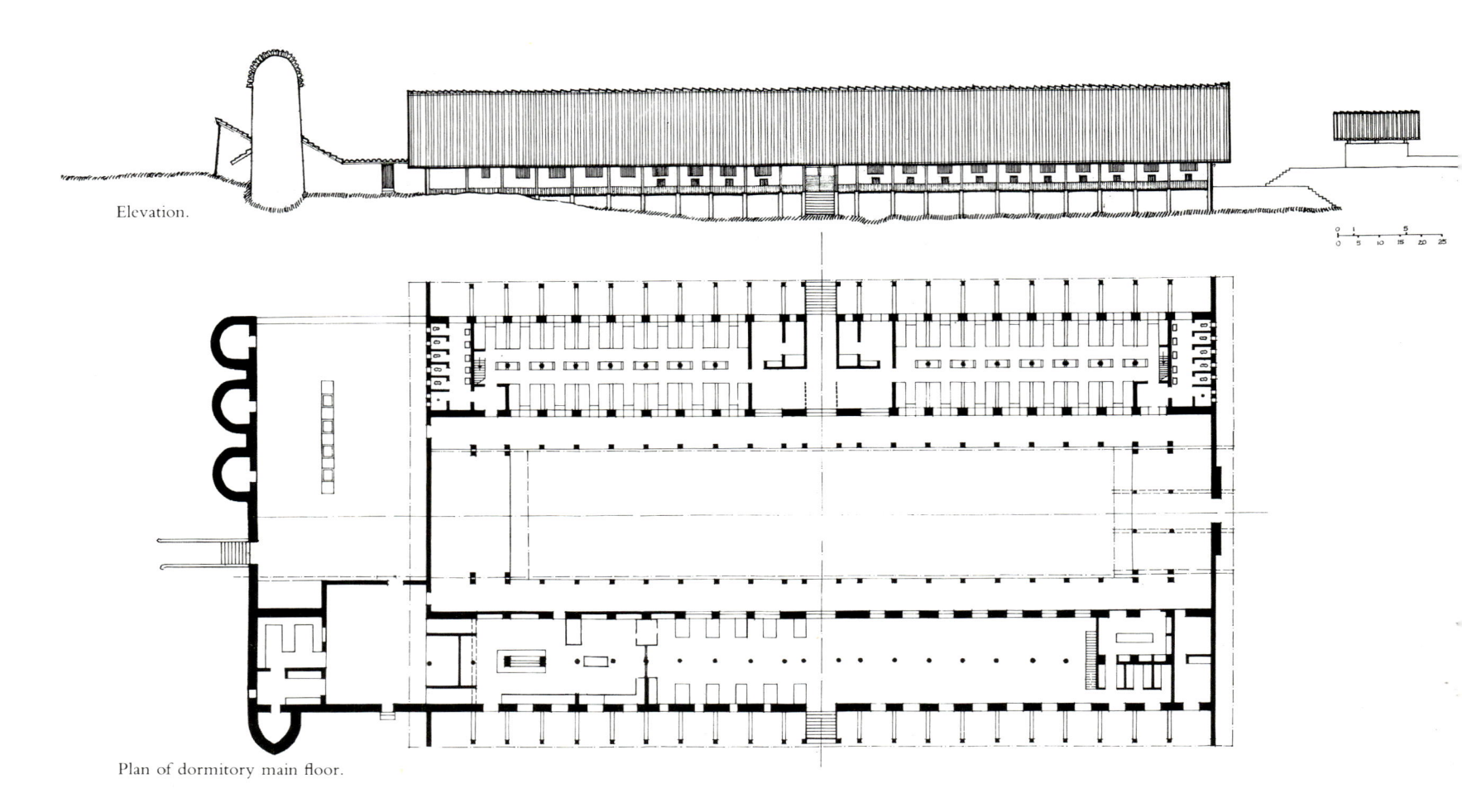

Elevation.

Plan of dormitory main floor.

Convent building seen from the main approach.

Front entrance to the Girls' Centre.

Kitchen and dining area of Girls' Centre.

SCHOOLS

SIDE ELEVATION

END ELEVATION

PLAN

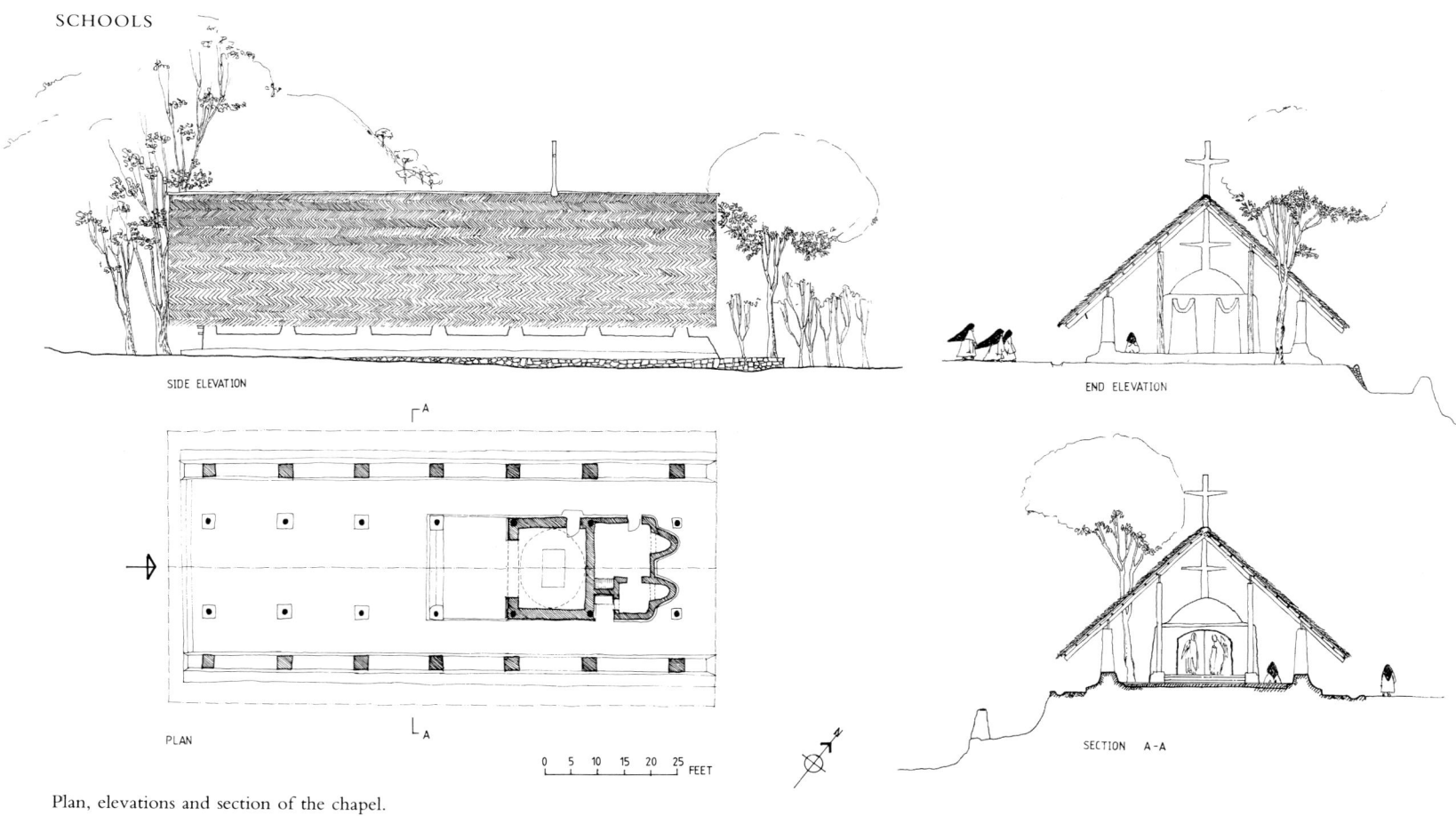

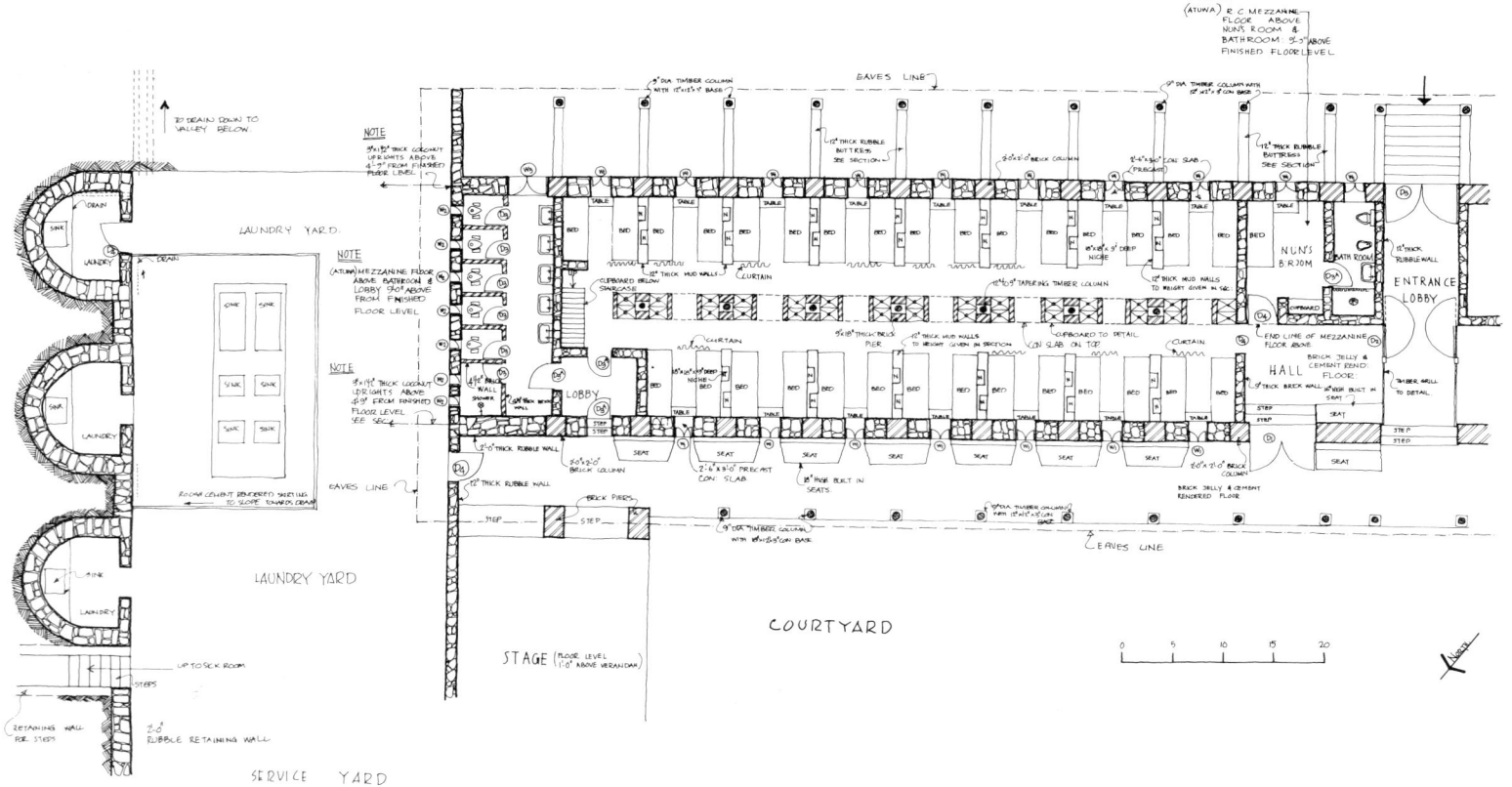

SECTION A-A

Plan, elevations and section of the chapel.

Partial floor plan of girls' dormitory.

FARM SCHOOL

View to the exterior from the dormitory lobby.

Laundry.

INTEGRAL EDUCATION CENTRE, PILIYANDALA

Section.

On a low hill by the Bolgoda Lake, this complex of buildings was intended as centre for adult education, occasional seminars on a variety of theological and secular subjects, and also as a holiday retreat. Run by the Catholic Church, it was financed by Misereor, a West German Roman Catholic aid-giving organisation, which had also helped the projects at Hanwella and Mahalpe.

The construction is simple and low-cost — brick walls and a timber-framed roof. It was built along the contours of the site except for the main all-purpose hall, which spans the central valley. A new, larger hall is now to be added. At the moment there are twenty bedrooms and a separate apartment for the resident project manager, plus accommodation for four general staff members, a library, the multi-purpose hall, and kitchens.

Buildings adapted to the terrain.

EDUCATION CENTRE

Site plan.

93

SCHOOLS

Detail of curved stair railing and low roofs.

Corridor.

UNIVERSITY OF RUHUNU, MATARA
ARTS AND SCIENCE FACULTIES

A spectacular site on the south coast overlooking the sea was chosen for the Arts and Science Faculties of an entirely new university. The initial intake of graduates was to grow to a total of four to five thousand in the coming years. There were superb views from almost every point of this site, and these became from the start an overwhelming influence on the planning — to accentuate certain views, frame others, give delight and surprise at every turn as one wound through buildings and landscape. The very fact of being at the university in these surroundings would be a beneficial addition to student life.

Entered almost at sea level, the site has three hills which rise to about 120 feet with valleys between. The hill nearest the beach was planned for residential buildings, the other two for the Arts and Science Faculties respectively, and the valley between the Arts and Science Faculties to be bridged by the library, the open air theatre (to accommodate 1,500, plus whomsoever could stand on the verandahs of overlooking buildings), and a coffee shop as social centre higher up the valley.

Technical aspects were carefully dealt with when planning the buildings. But in addition, covered links were built to give passage and space for pause, contemplation, and the meeting of minds, whether contemplative or active, and thus gazebos, pavilions and verandahs were very much part of the essential concept.

Partial view of the faculty buildings.

RUHUNU UNIVERSITY

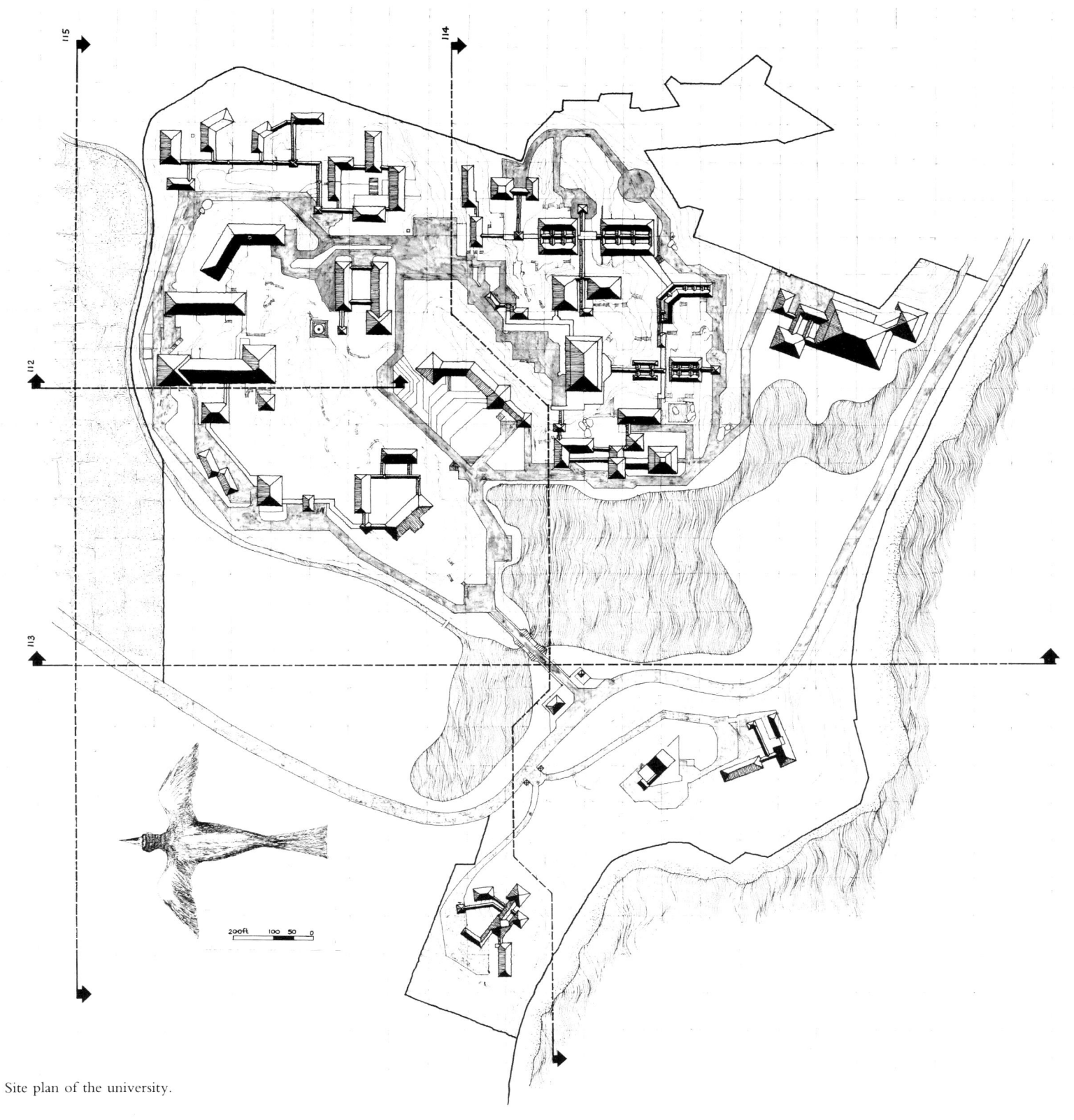

Site plan of the university.

Physics I building (left), Physics lecture hall (right) and water tank pavilion (centre).

Physics lecture hall viewed from Physics building. Water tank pavilion in the distance.

Water tank pavilion (left) and roof of Physics complex.

Physics building columns seen through a slit window.

SCHOOLS

Physics building seen from the top-level corner of Chemistry 1 building.

Columns at corner of Chemistry I building. Zoology faculty in distance.

SCHOOLS

Single storey Chemistry II building (left) with roofs of Botany and Zoology (right).

Link in the Arts Faculty.

Overleaf: View of the Science Faculty from verandah of Philosophy building.

Detail of Chemistry II (left) and I (right) buildings.

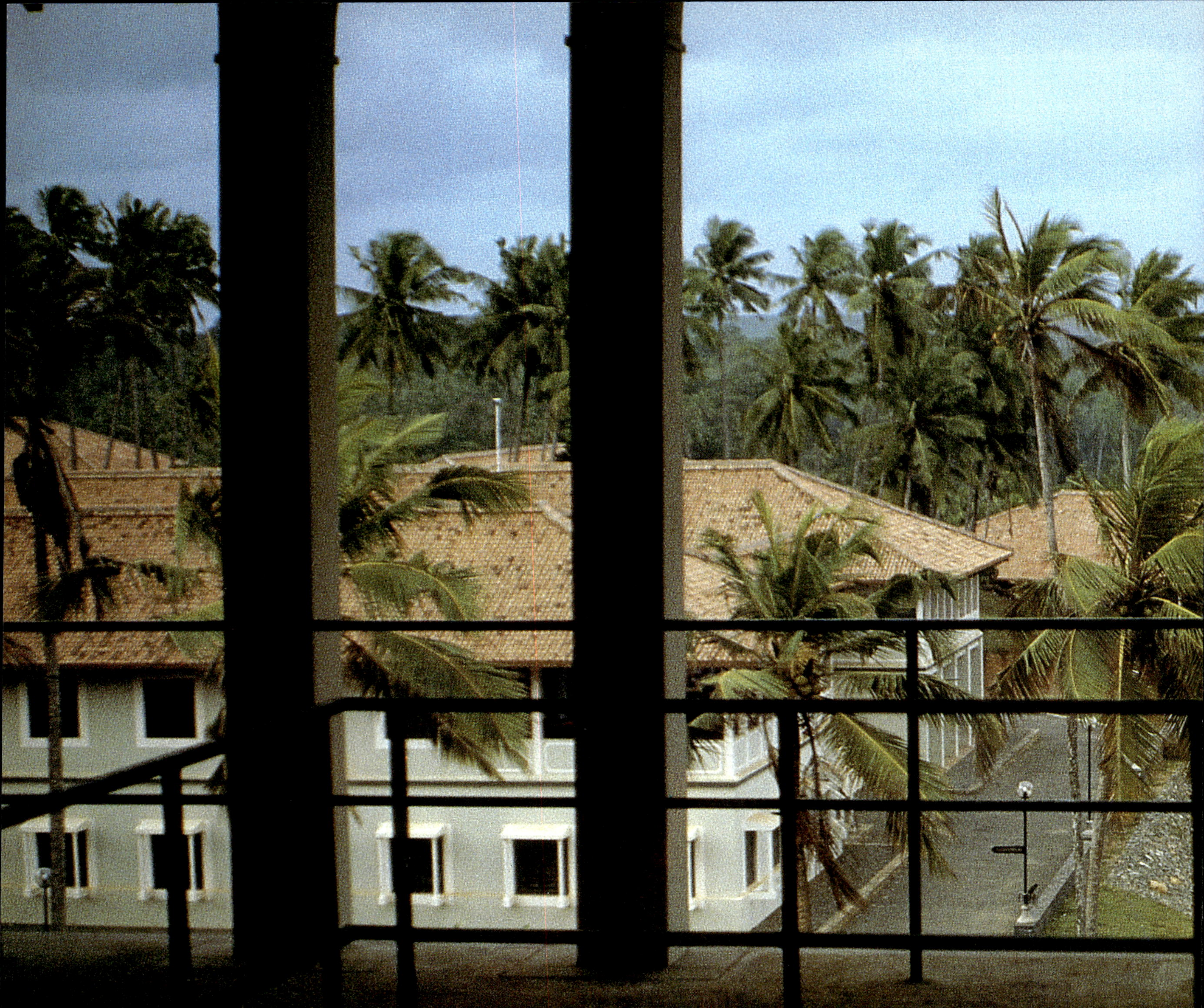

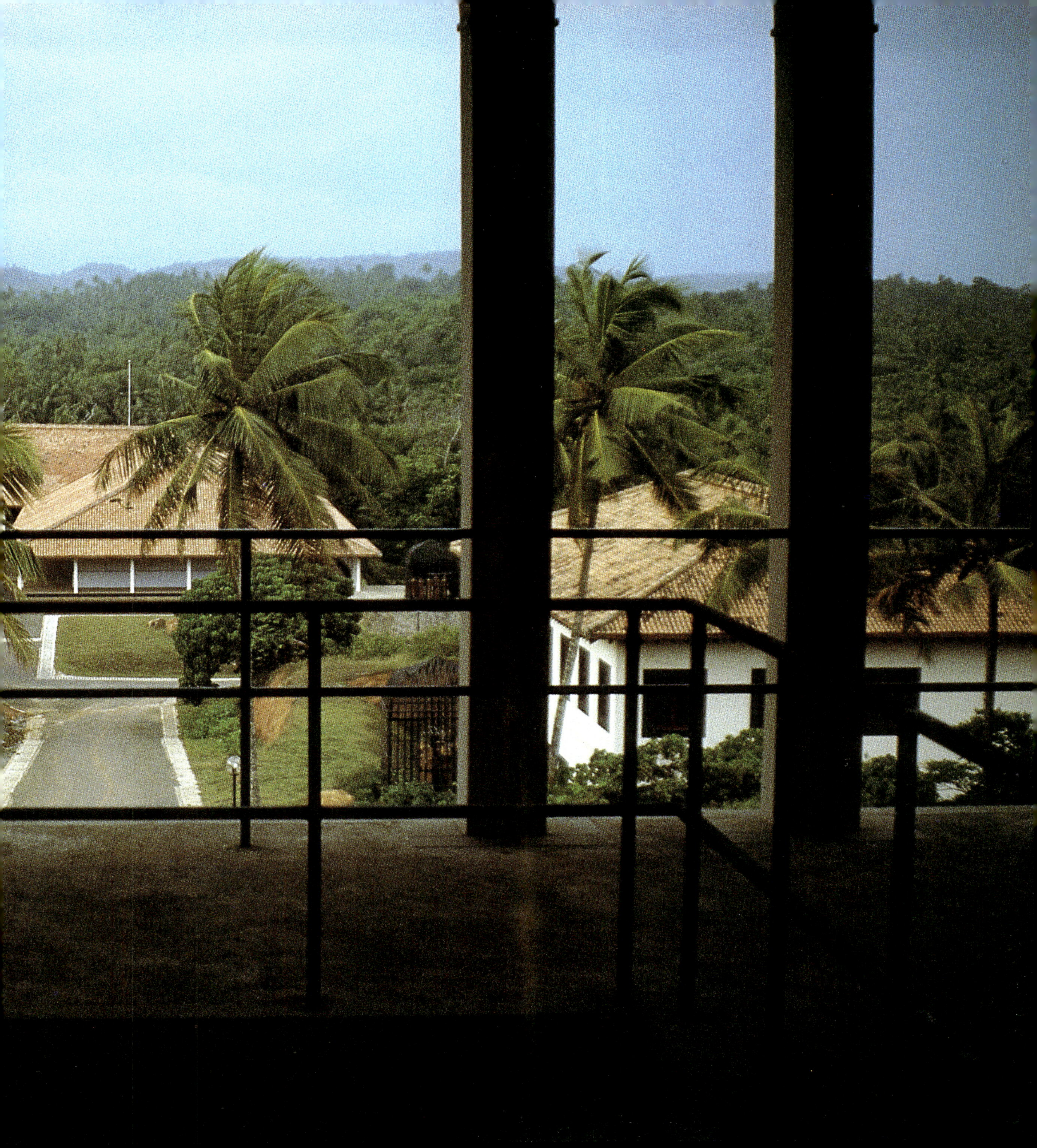

Lower link corridor from tutorial rooms to Philosophy building.

Upper link from pavilion to tutorial rooms.

OFFICES

THE ARCHITECT'S OFFICE, COLOMBO

STEEL CORPORATION OFFICE, ORUWELA

AGRARIAN RESEARCH AND TRAINING INSTITUTE, COLOMBO

THE ARCHITECT'S OFFICE, COLOMBO

The office had originally been planned as a doctor's house, but by the time the foundations had grown to ground level he had decided to stay where he was and Bawa was able to buy the property and to convert it into an office. Thus, the original spaces were transformed to suit the architect's convenience: kitchen into accounts office, quantity surveying in the pantry, the three upstairs bedrooms into one main drawing room — lying between the two courtyards — into the main meeting room and Bawa's office.

The general progression of spaces, first through the entrance courtyard then through the central court and finally into the great space of the meeting room and the architect's office, establishes a mood which can easily be felt and which would then set the temper of acceptance or rejection — a great advantage for an architectural practice.

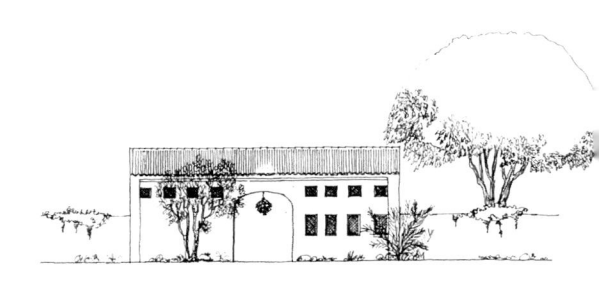

Street elevation.

Entrance facade to offices.

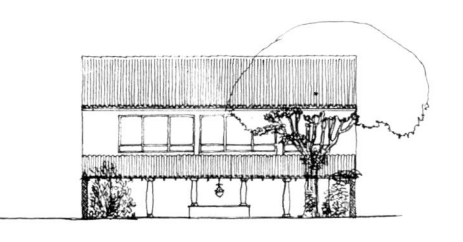

Garden elevation of Bawa's office.

Entrance pool seen laterally.

ARCHITECT'S OFFICE

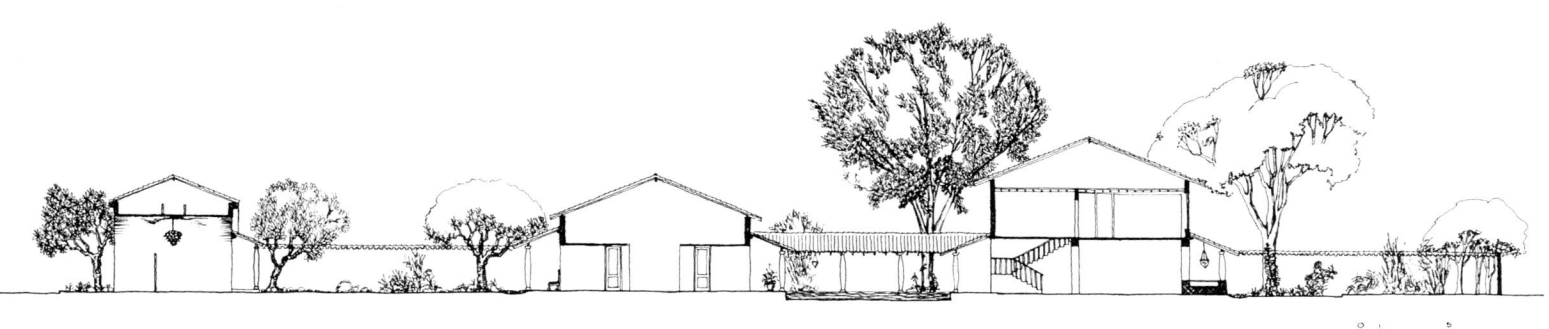

Longitudinal section.

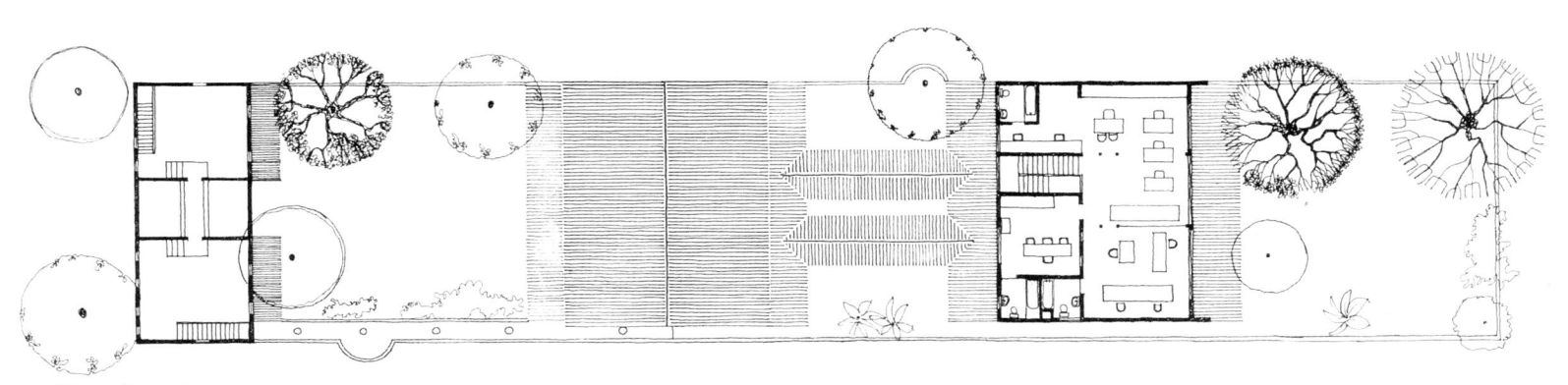

Upper floor plan.

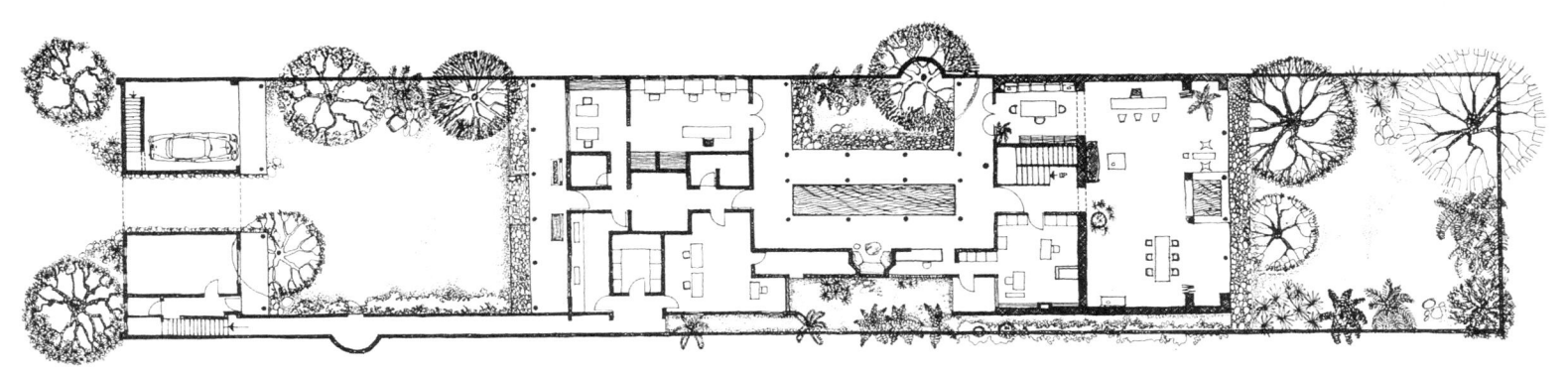

Ground floor plan.

Overleaf: Entrance courtyard to architect's office.

115

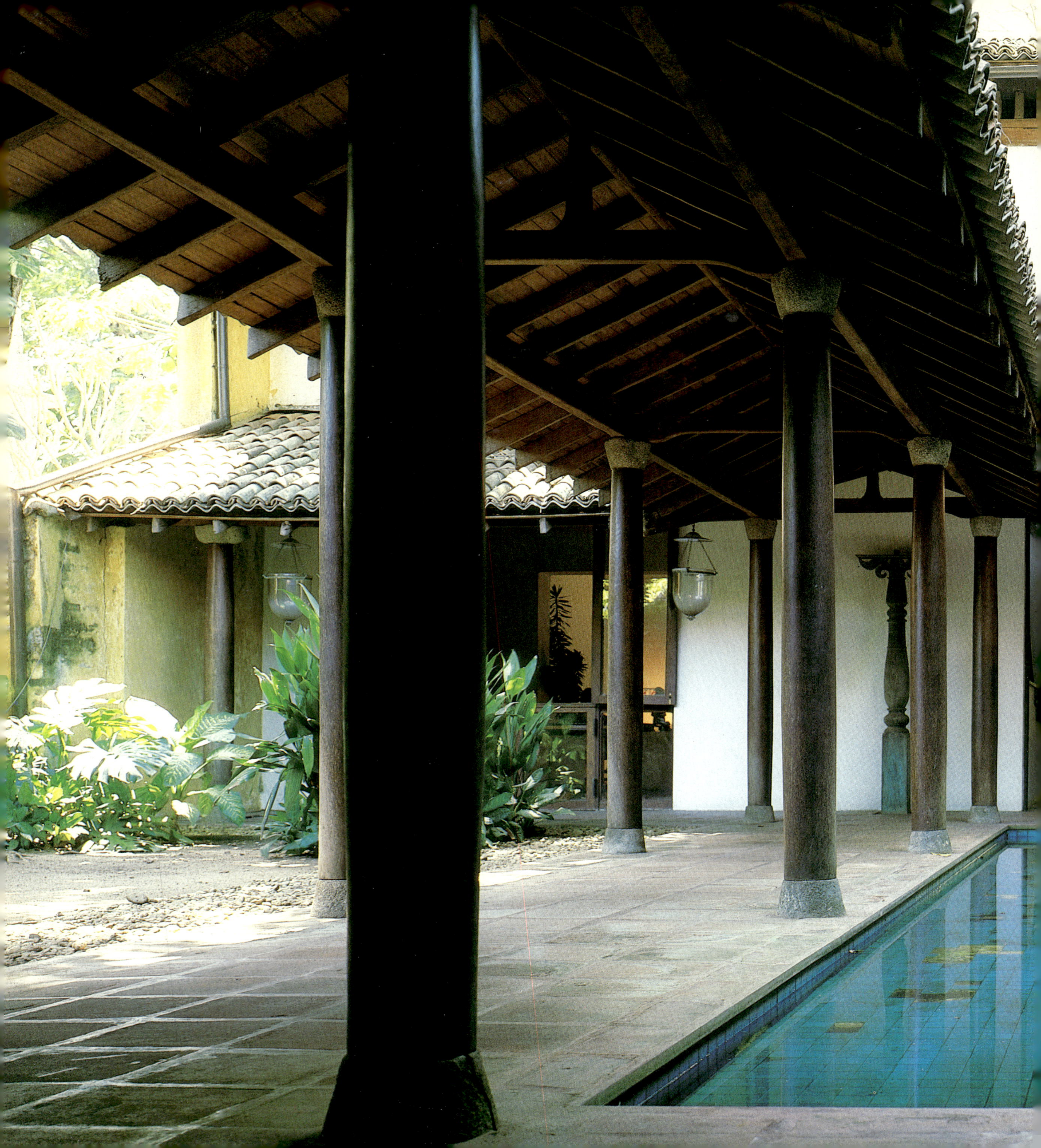

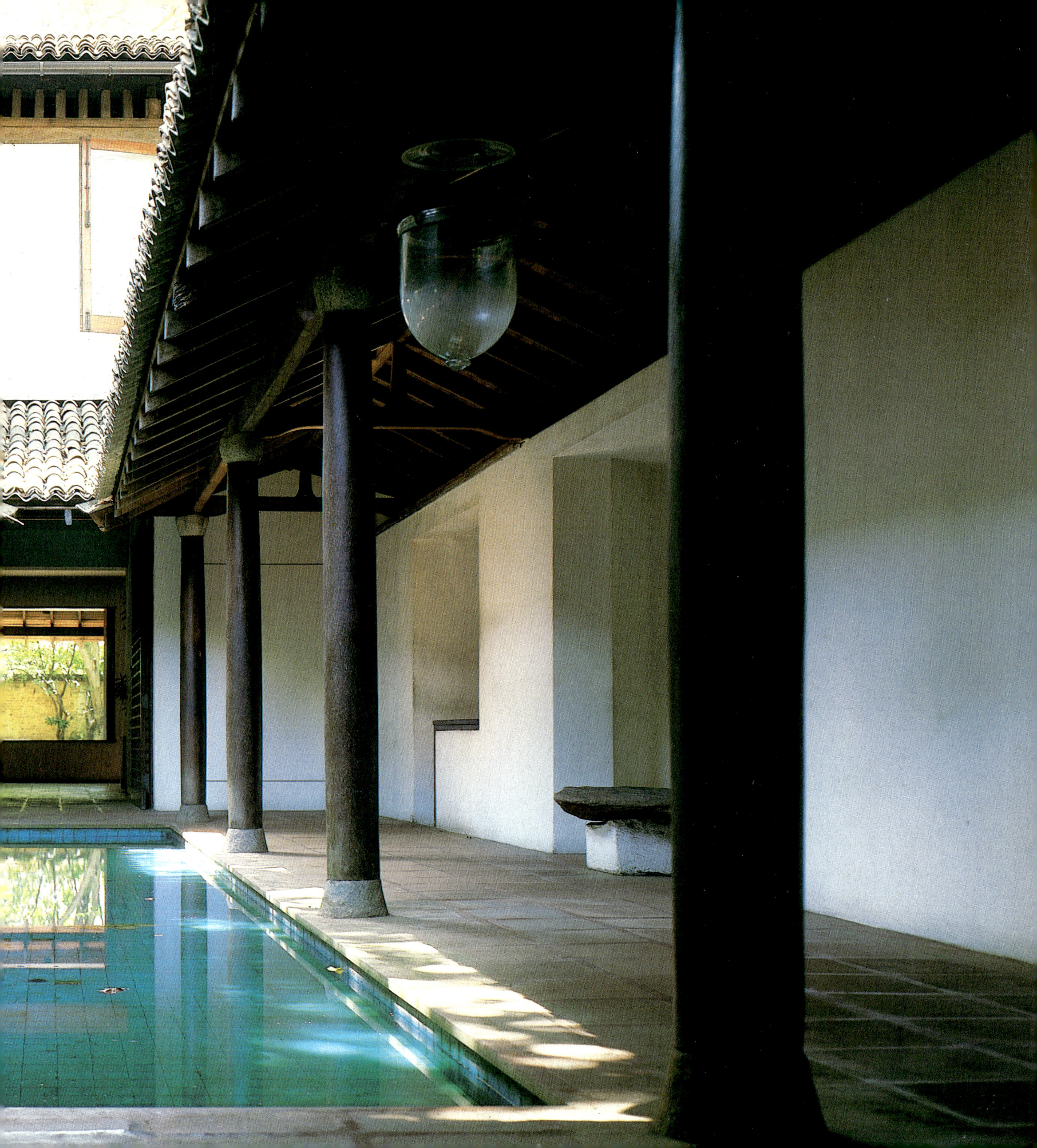

OFFICES

View from the courtyard.

ARCHITECT'S OFFICE

Architect's office and conference area.

Architect's office, verandah and courtyard.

STEEL CORPORATION OFFICE, ORUWELA

The office that was to be built against the great bulk of the steel rolling mill, required a gentler and more human scale. It had however to make its presence felt as the hub and administrative centre of the mill. This was achieved by a simple rectangular plan, with disciplined elevations of precast perforated and windowed walls and emphatic proportions to set it in scale with the mill building.

Set at a ninety degree angle to the mill, the building lies half on land and half on water, with the lower ground floor two feet above the level of the water in the huge pond which is used for steel production necessities and is always kept at this level. Reinforced concrete throughout, it is a frame structure with the panel infilling made up of a precast grill of rectangular openings. The scale of these perforated panels diminishes from floor to floor and the entrance door of wood takes up an entire panel.

Office wing and mill (right) seen from across the pond.

Facade with entrance to the offices.

STEEL CORPORATION OFFICE

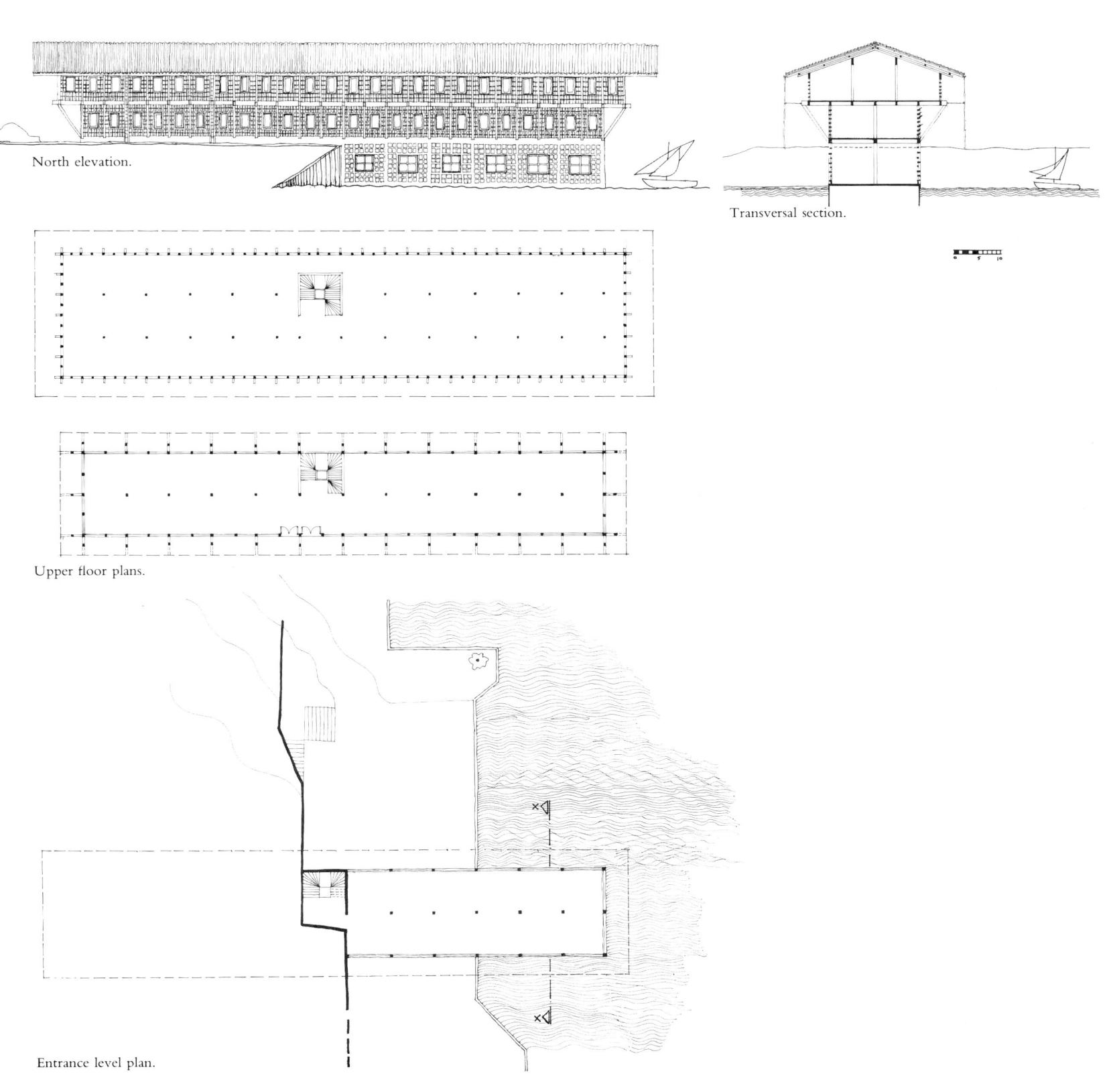

North elevation.

Transversal section.

Upper floor plans.

Entrance level plan.

AGRARIAN RESEARCH AND TRAINING INSTITUTE, COLOMBO

This office building was the first to be built in a wholly residential area, and it was necessary to keep its scale and feeling in sympathy with the environment. It was also an opportunity to show that such an office could be used with greater efficiency, and pleasure, and be better cared for by its users, than the conventional office buildings which took their patterns from abroad.

Thus corridors are single stacked with open courtyards in between. The courtyards are now well planted, and ventilation and light are excellent in all the office spaces.

Porte cochère entrance to the institute.

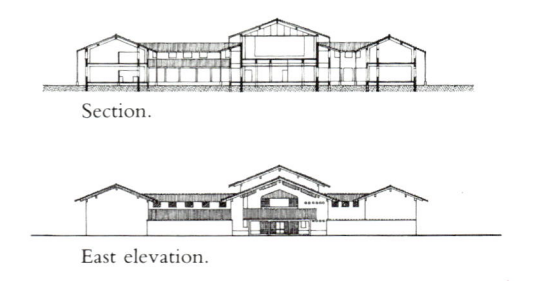

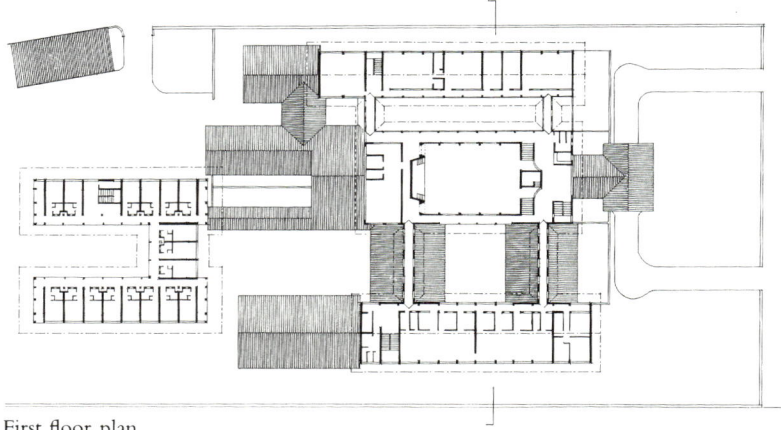

Section.

East elevation.

First floor plan.

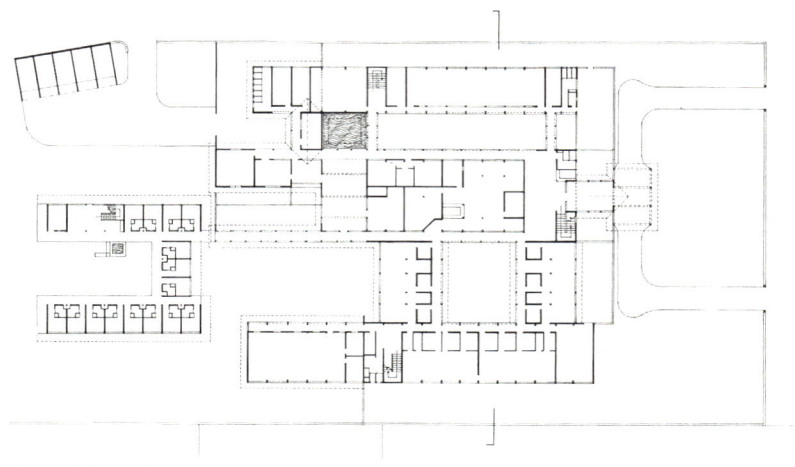

Ground floor plan.

TRAINING INSTITUTE

Inner courtyard.

First floor corridor.

OFFICES

View across an internal courtyard.

HOTELS

BENTOTA BEACH HOTEL, BENTOTA

PANAMA HOTEL, PANAMA

CLUB VILLA, BENTOTA

TRITON HOTEL, AHUNGALLA

SERENDIB HOTEL, BENTOTA

BENTOTA BEACH HOTEL, BENTOTA

Bentota Beach was one of the first tourist hotels to be built in Sri Lanka. Originally, it was to have a limited number of bedrooms, thirty, and very large public spaces, as a place to which shipping agents could take large groups of passengers who spent a day in Sri Lanka on the England-Australia run when ships passed daily through the port of Colombo.

With the closure of the Suez Canal this stopped, so more bedrooms were added to make the enterprise more viable. Later, the number of rooms was again increased, but the new wings of rooms were kept low so as not to lessen the importance of the original block, which stood dominant on its site between river and sea.

Elevation as seen from the beach.

View of the hotel from the beach.

BENTOTA BEACH HOTEL

Interior courtyard with pool.

HOTELS

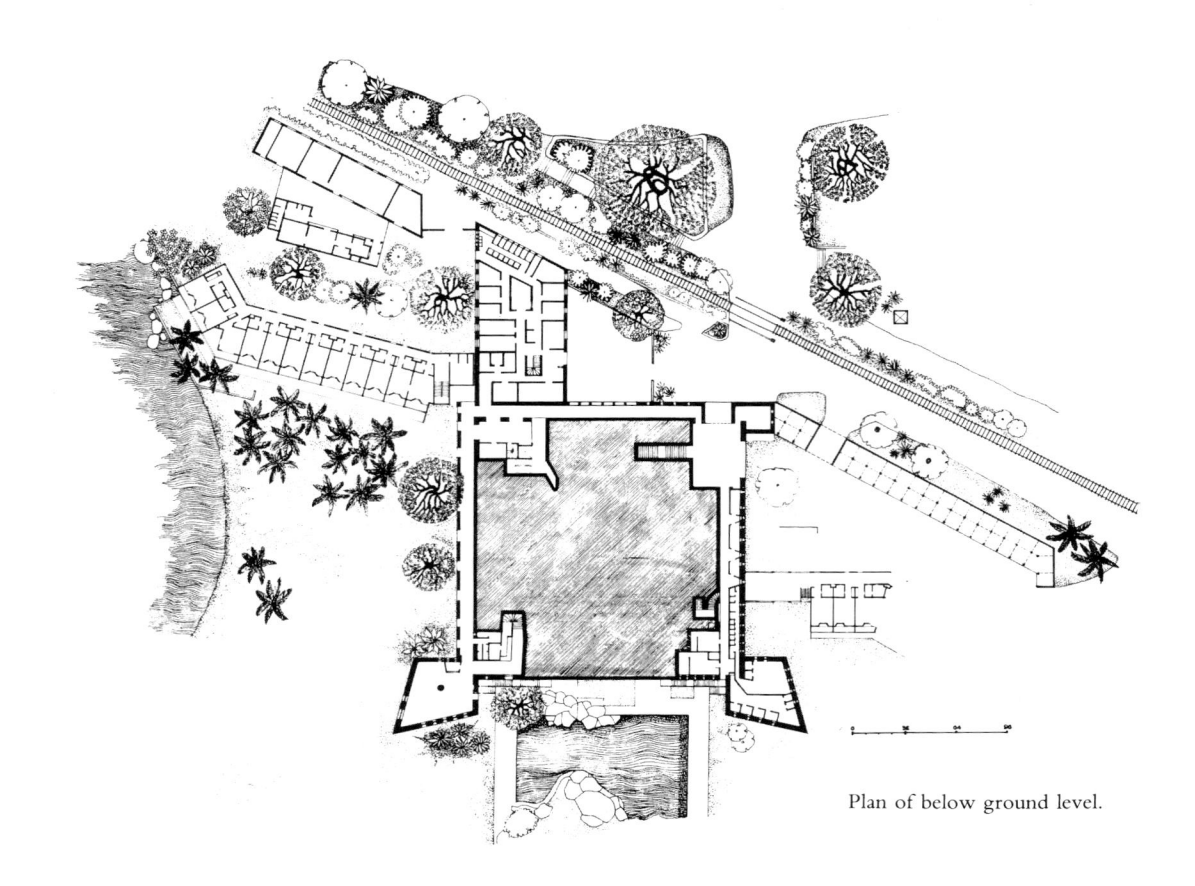

Plan of below ground level.

Porte cochère entrance.

BENTOTA BEACH HOTEL

Main entrance stairs and batik ceiling decoration.

Lobby.

HOTELS

Section.

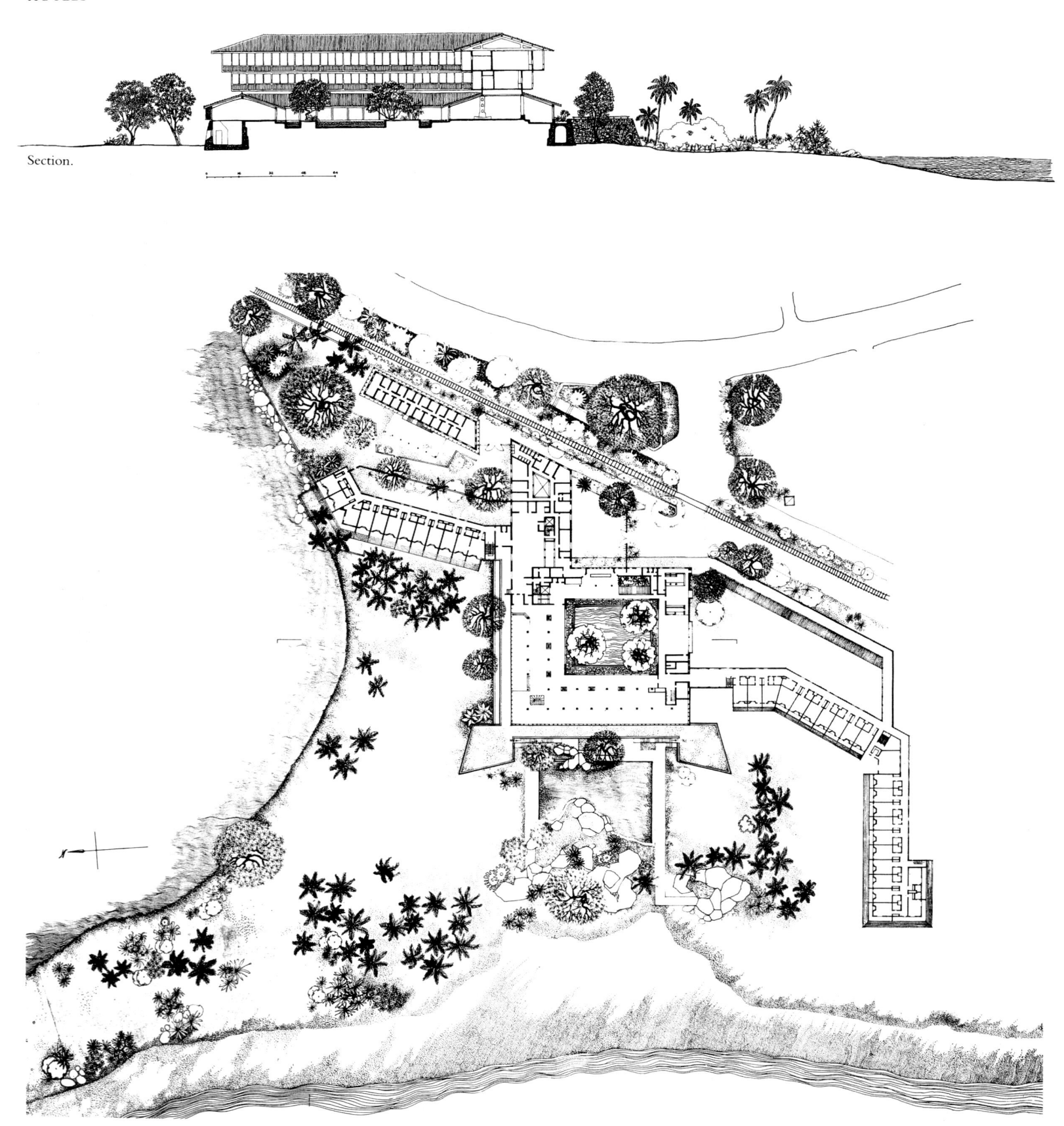

Plan of main (lobby) floor.

Detail of southwest corner facade.

View from an upper balcony.

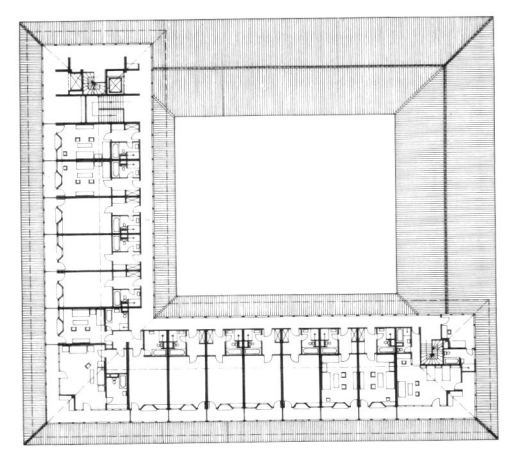

First floor plan.

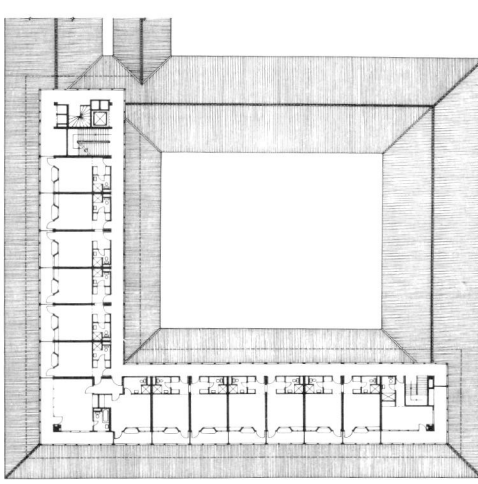

Second floor plan.

PANAMA HOTEL, PANAMA

This was to be a new pattern for a tourist hotel in Sri Lanka, using streets as corridors and treating each room or two as a separate unit — like a small town or village with houses, assembly rooms, restaurants, barbecues, shops — all the elements that go into making a small, closely integrated town — with, in addition, a boat jetty and pier, swimming pools, stables and garages.

The site was on the east coast of Sri Lanka and adjoined the Yala Wild Life Sanctuary. The project even went as far as the commencement of building when, although it had been given the sanction of the Sri Lanka Tourist Board, the Government was pressurised by wild life conservationists to stop any hotel construction in proximity to the Wild Life Sanctuaries. It is ironic though that now the two units of one of the planned terrace of rooms has been used as the nucleus of a totally unplanned development of low-grade tourist accommodation which, uncontrolled as it was unauthorised, constitutes a much greater danger to the area. The site lay south of the village Panama, a spit of land between the lagoon and the sea — extremely beautiful.

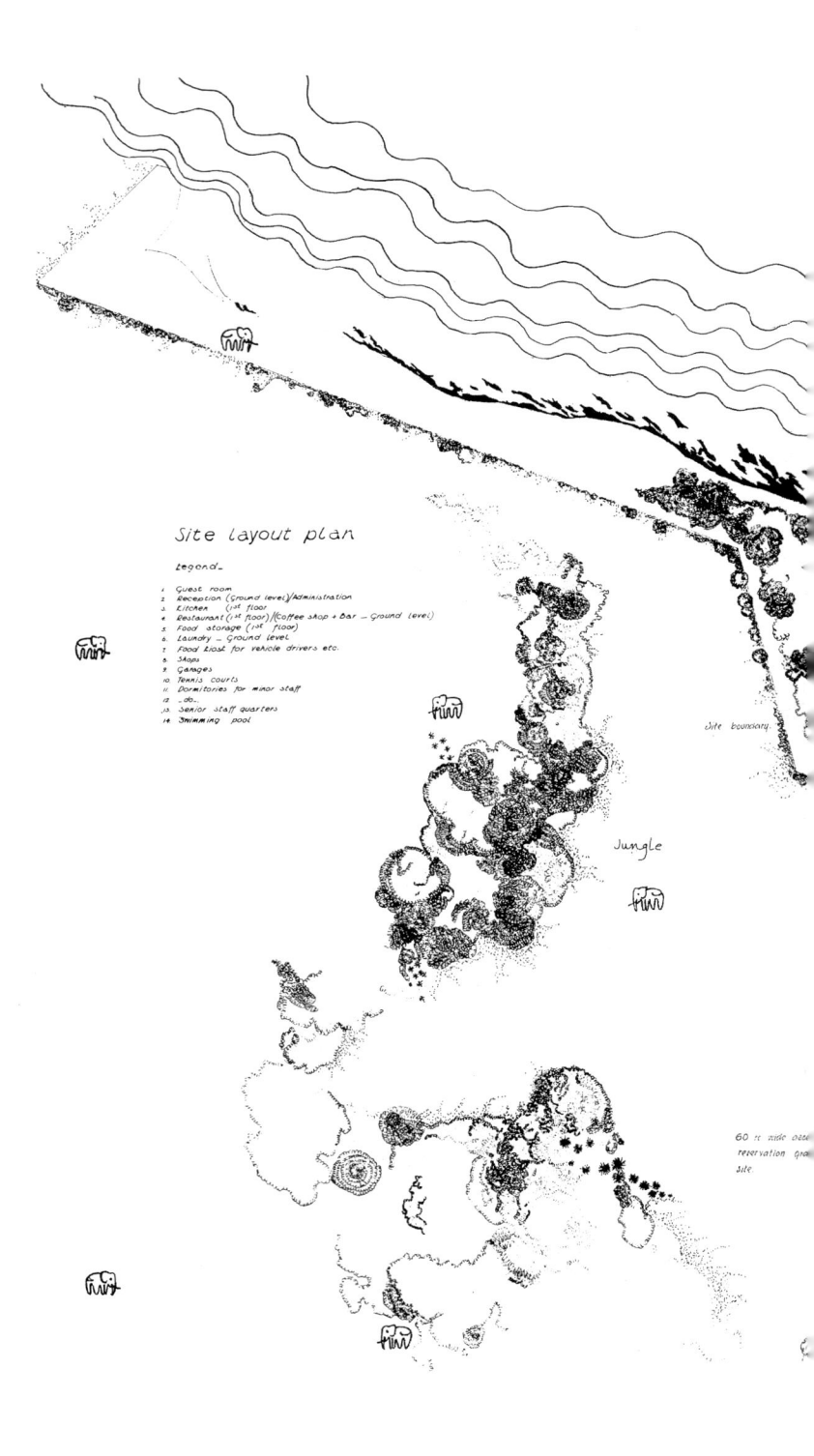

Site plan of project and locational map of Sri Lanka.

PANAMA HOTEL

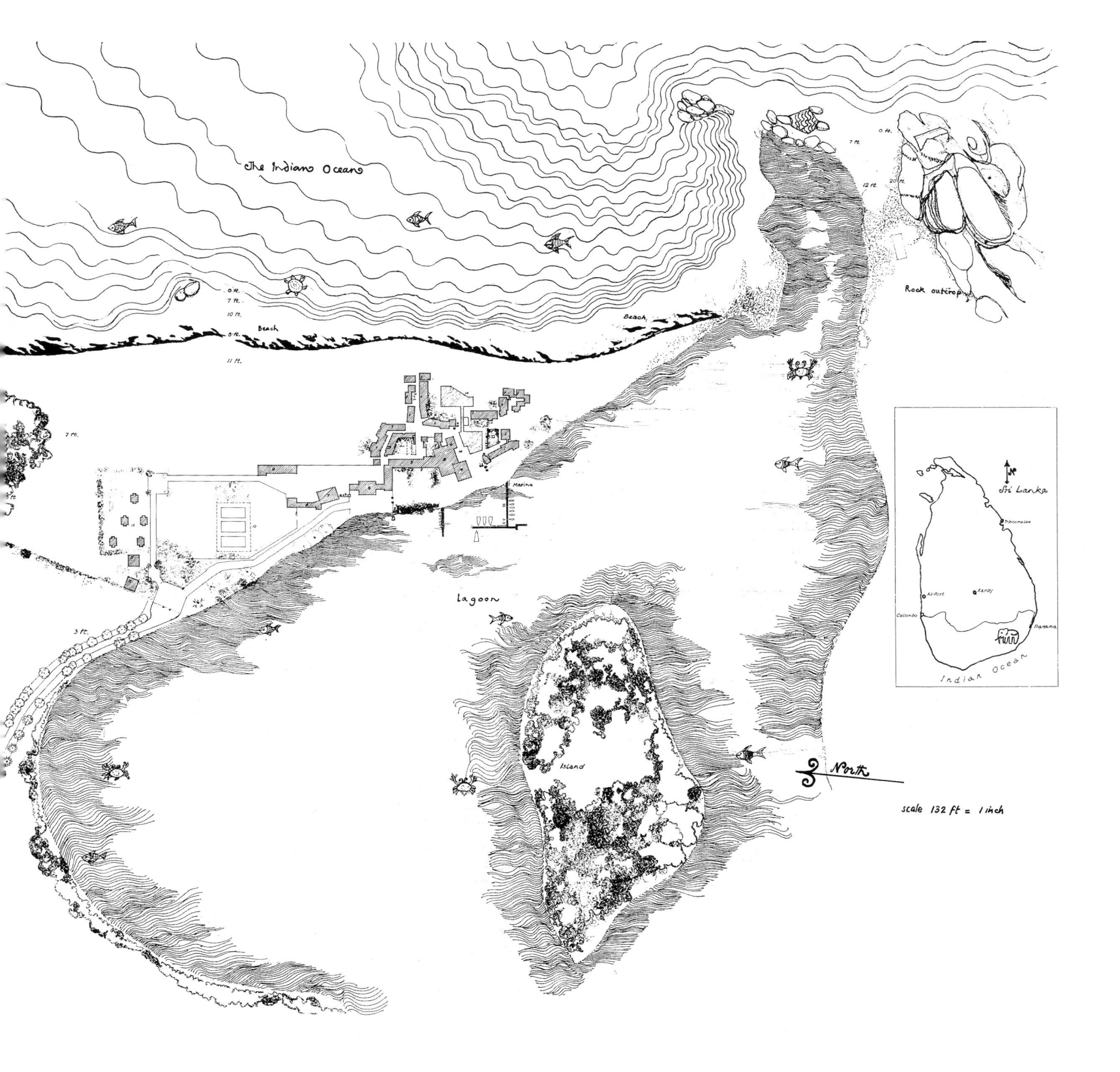

HOTELS

Ground floor plan of the entire complex.

PANAMA HOTEL

Ground floor plan

Legend
101–179 Guest rooms

1. Light/Ventilation shaft
2. Boat equipment store/or shop
3. Furniture store
4. Referigiration Plant room
5. Food lift and service access to kitchen on 1st floor
6. Pump house
7. Female staff changing room lockers & toilets
8. Male staff changing room lockers & toilets
9. Delivery lay-by & temporary store
10. House keepers stores
11. –do–
12. House keepers' office
13–16 Laundry
17. Linen room
18. Common living room for staff
19a–19g Senior staff bed rooms
20. Staff toilets
21. Managers' office
22–23 Linen rooms
24. Pool machinery house
25. Toilets for shops (H & I)
A to I Shops – 9 nos

27–29 Minor staff canteen, kitchen & stores
30. Courtyard
31. Toilets for shops & canteen
32. Vehicle drivers' food kiosk

North

HOTELS

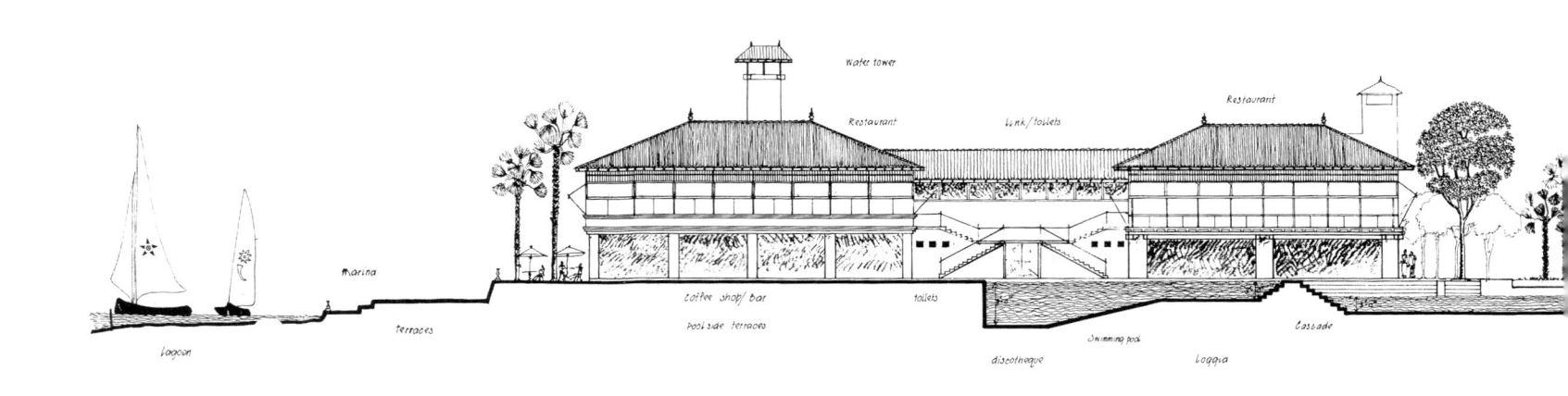

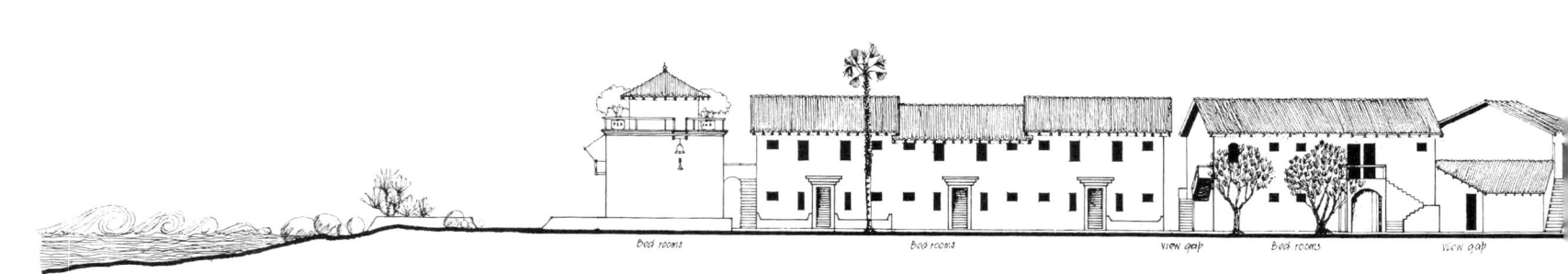

Sections through reception lobby and swimming pool.

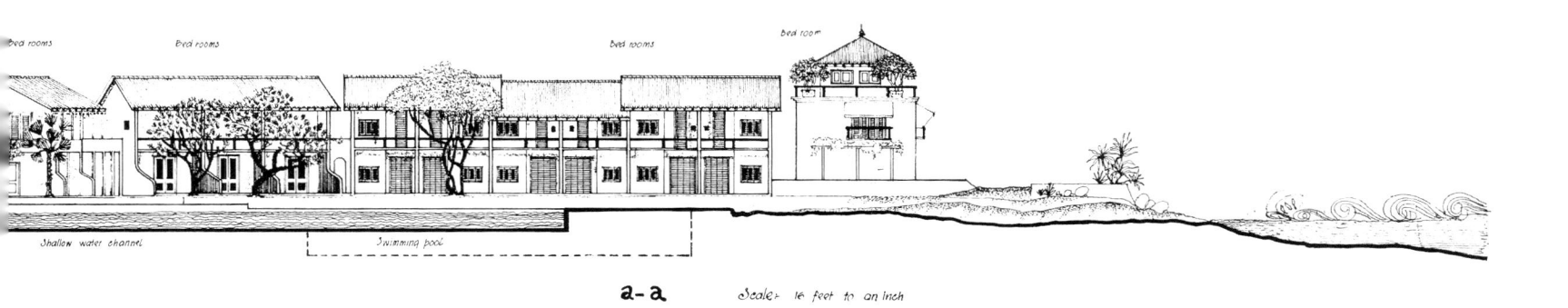

PANAMA HOTEL

Bed rooms · Bed rooms · Bed rooms · Bed room

Shallow water channel · Swimming pool

a-a Scale: 16 feet to an inch

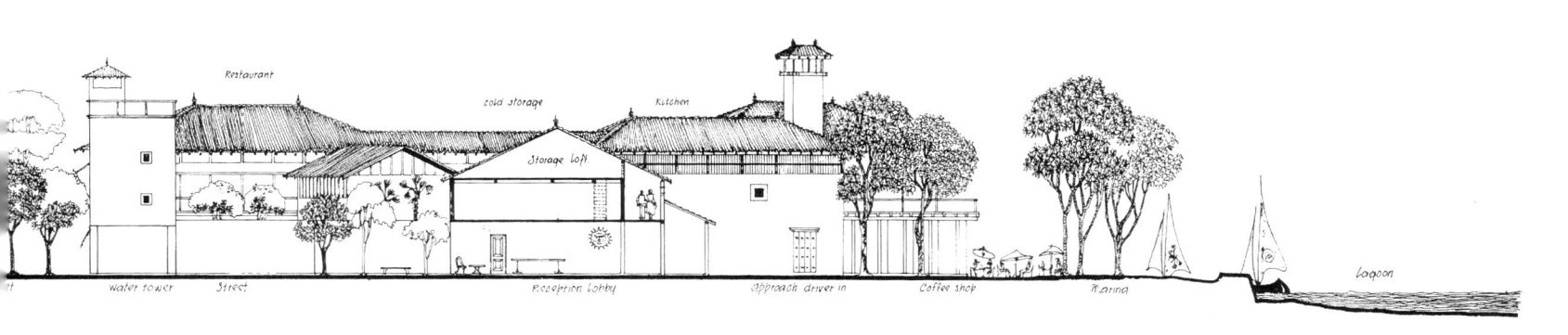

Restaurant · cold storage · Kitchen

water tower · Street · Storage loft · Reception Lobby · Approach drive in · Coffee shop · Marina · Lagoon

b-b Scale: 16 feet to an inch

CLUB VILLA, BENTOTA

The original house on the beach at Bentota was built about 1880 but fell into almost total ruin. The two-storeyed block containing some bedrooms was the only part left intact, and was bought in 1979. To this was added the loggia and courtyard, and bedrooms and kitchens of the present house, and a swimming pool was built in the courtyard.

View of the west facade from the beach.

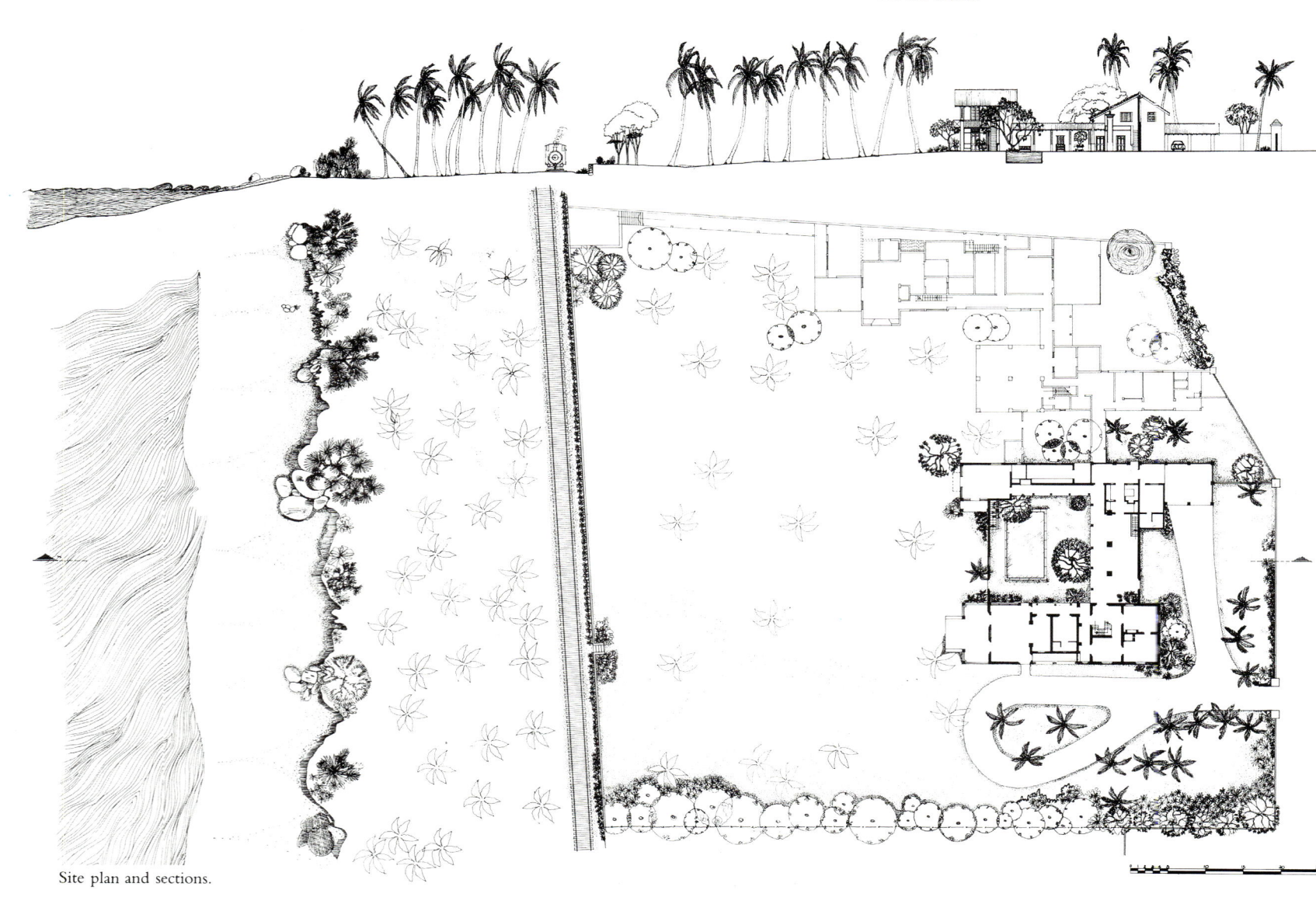

Site plan and sections.

Club Villa
Bentota

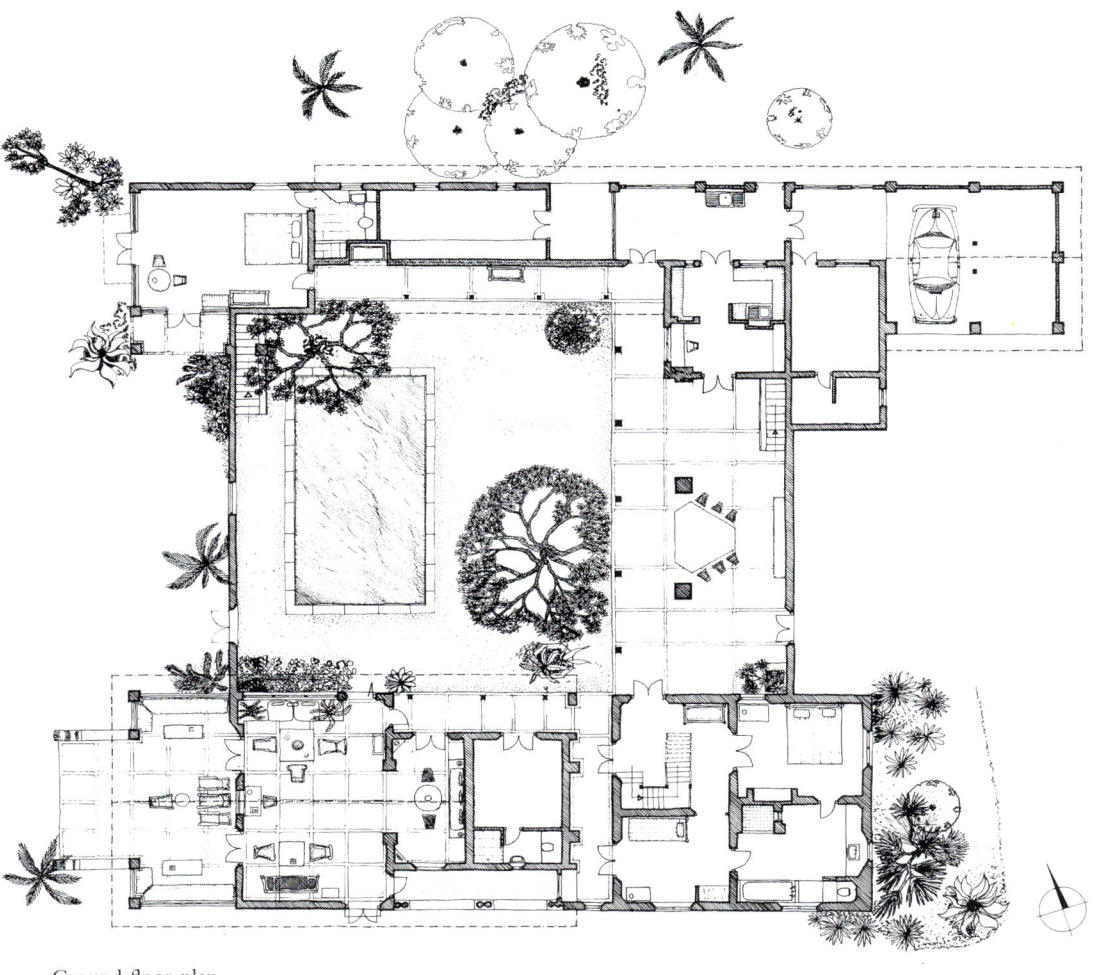

Ground floor plan.

Loggia and courtyard seen from the southeast corner.

139

TRITON HOTEL, AHUNGALLA

The planning of this hotel was largely shaped by the site. A long narrow beach front reached by an equally long narrow strip of land which gave the hotel access from the main Colombo-Galle Road. This long approach provided the opportunity of dramatising the arrival with a view of the sea across a large reflecting pool, then a polished lobby floor, and finally the swimming pool and the sea, all essentially at the same level. At the entrance portico the same illusion was kept — the swimming pool ending, without a visual break, at the waves on the beach. The lobby, coffee shop, lounge and pool are designed as linked open pavilions, all with the wide view of the sea dominating.

In the same way, to emphasise the view, the first and second floor lobbies have the same extremely open vista of the beach and sea.

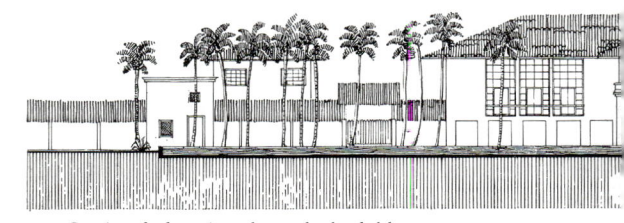

Sectional elevation through the lobby.

Entrance facade detail with coconut-tree pool in foreground.

Aerial view of the entire hotel and beachscape.

TRITON HOTEL

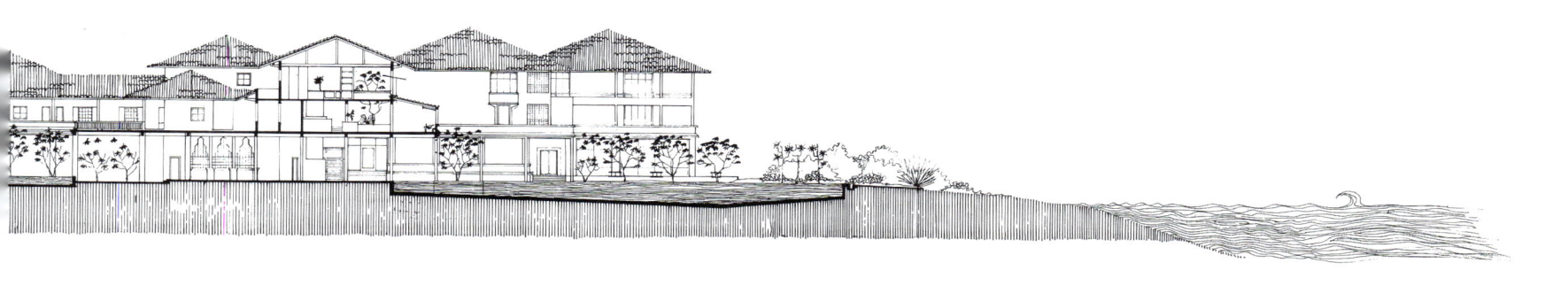

From the lobby to the pool to the sea.

141

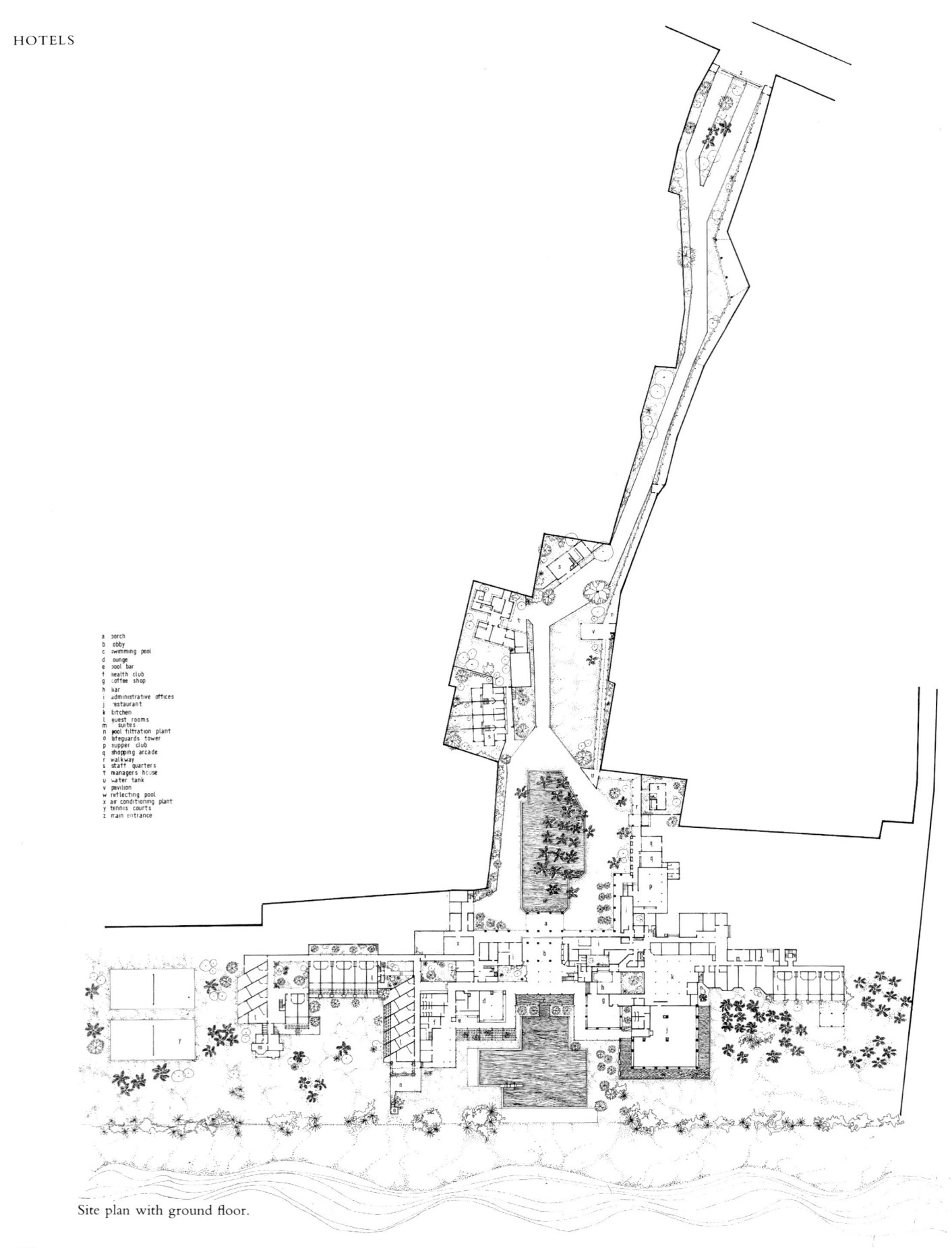

HOTELS

a   porch
b   lobby
c   swimming pool
d   lounge
e   pool bar
f   health club
g   coffee shop
h   bar
i   administrative offices
j   restaurant
k   kitchen
l   guest rooms
m   suites
n   pool filtration plant
o   lifeguards tower
p   supper club
q   shopping arcade
r   walkway
s   staff quarters
t   managers house
u   water tank
v   pavilion
w   reflecting pool
x   air conditioning plant
y   tennis courts
z   main entrance

Site plan with ground floor.

142

TRITON HOTEL

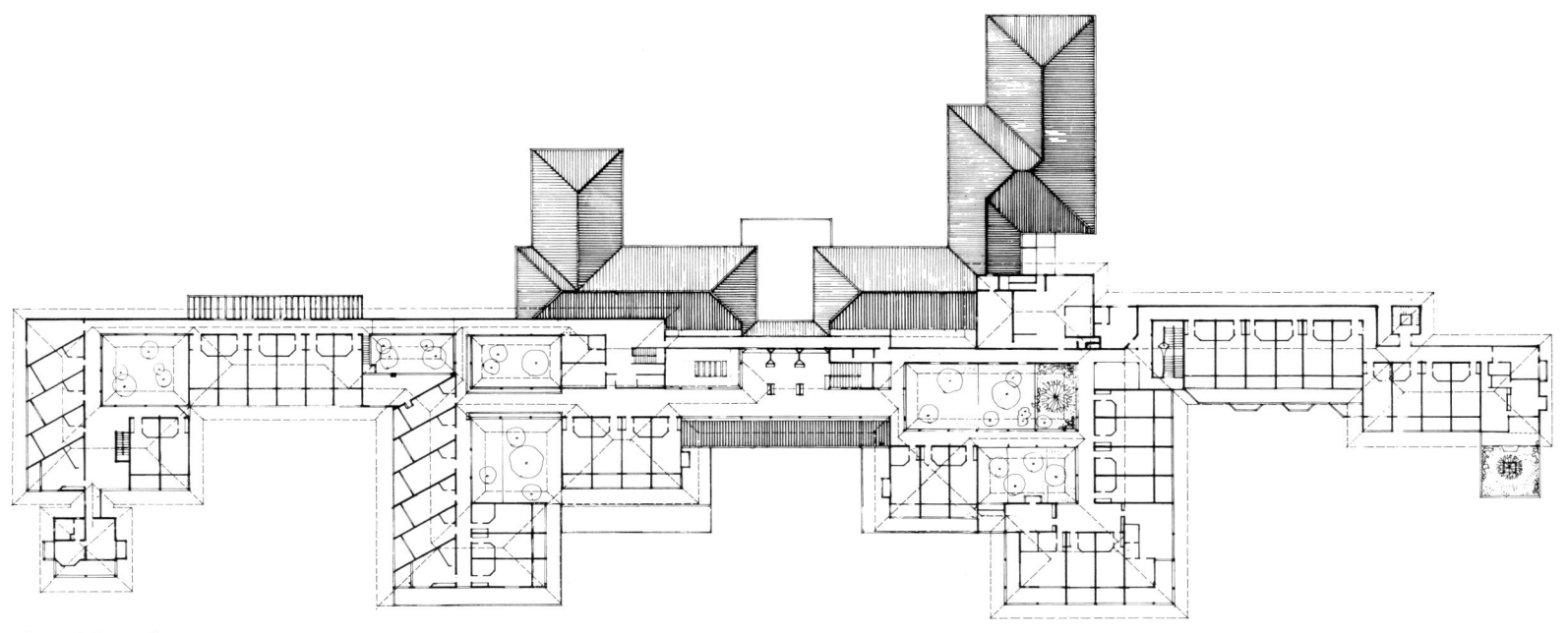

Second floor plan.

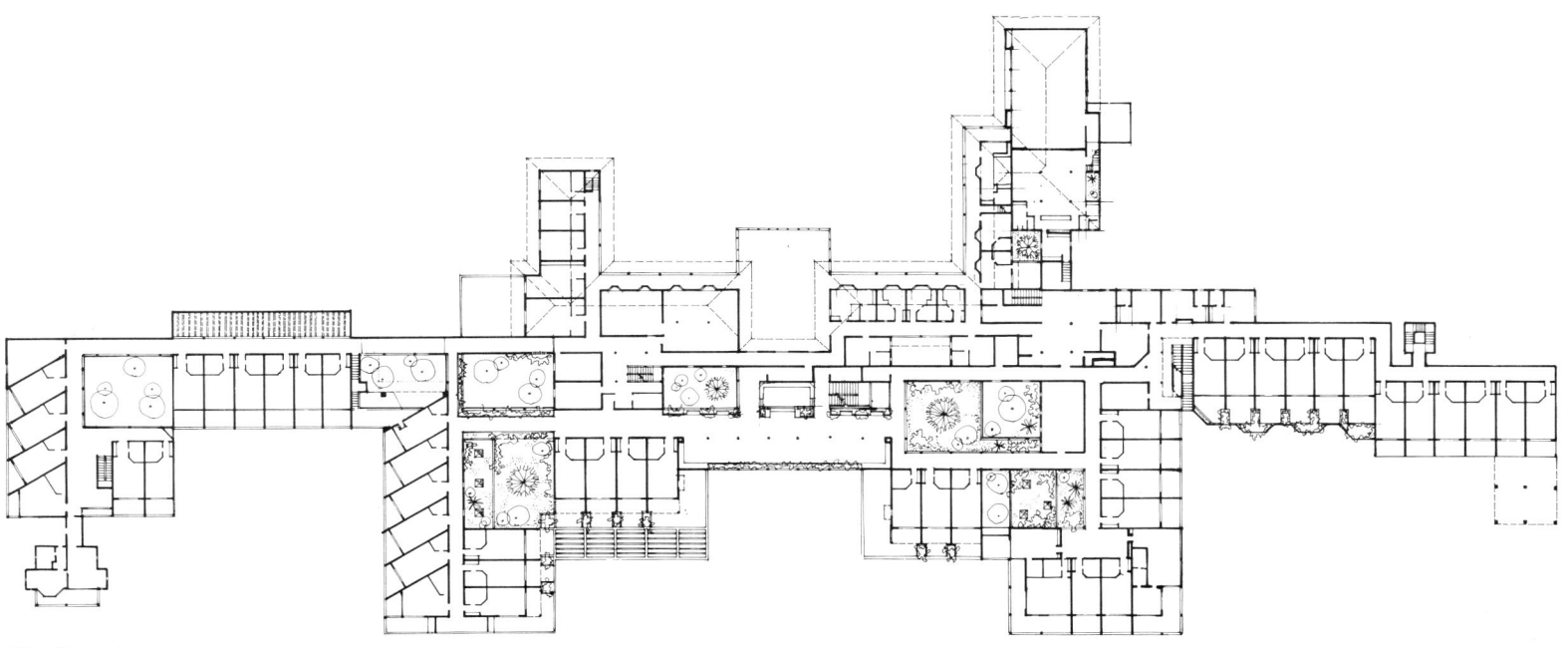

First floor plan.

HOTELS

Reception desk.

Rest area.

Lobby area around the pool.

Staircase to upper level.

Pool view westward from lobby across the pool to the sea.

TRITON HOTEL

View of the bar area and pool.

Upper-level lounge.

Second floor bridge and planted courtyards.

HOTELS

Glimpses of the sea and pool.

Shadows of trees along the walkway.

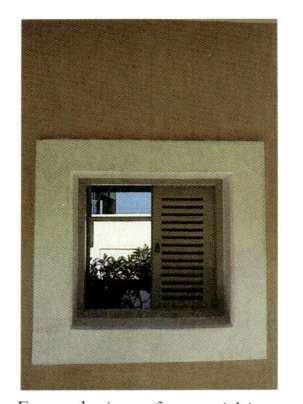

Framed views from within the hotel.

Second floor view of the pool, beach and sea.

View of the west facade facing the sea.

SERENDIB HOTEL, BENTOTA

Built at approximately the same time and next door to the Bentota Beach, the Serendib Hotel was not intended to be in the same luxury class. It started with twenty bedrooms, and was then built up in stages from the original twenty to the present one hundred bedrooms. Additional public spaces became necessary and were integrated into the wider planning. The beach front at Serendib is tremendously long and the hotel stretches its full length making the beach and the lawn between the rooms and the sea the most extensively used area — an in effect open-air public room.

Rooms and open corridors around courtyards.

View from the beach.

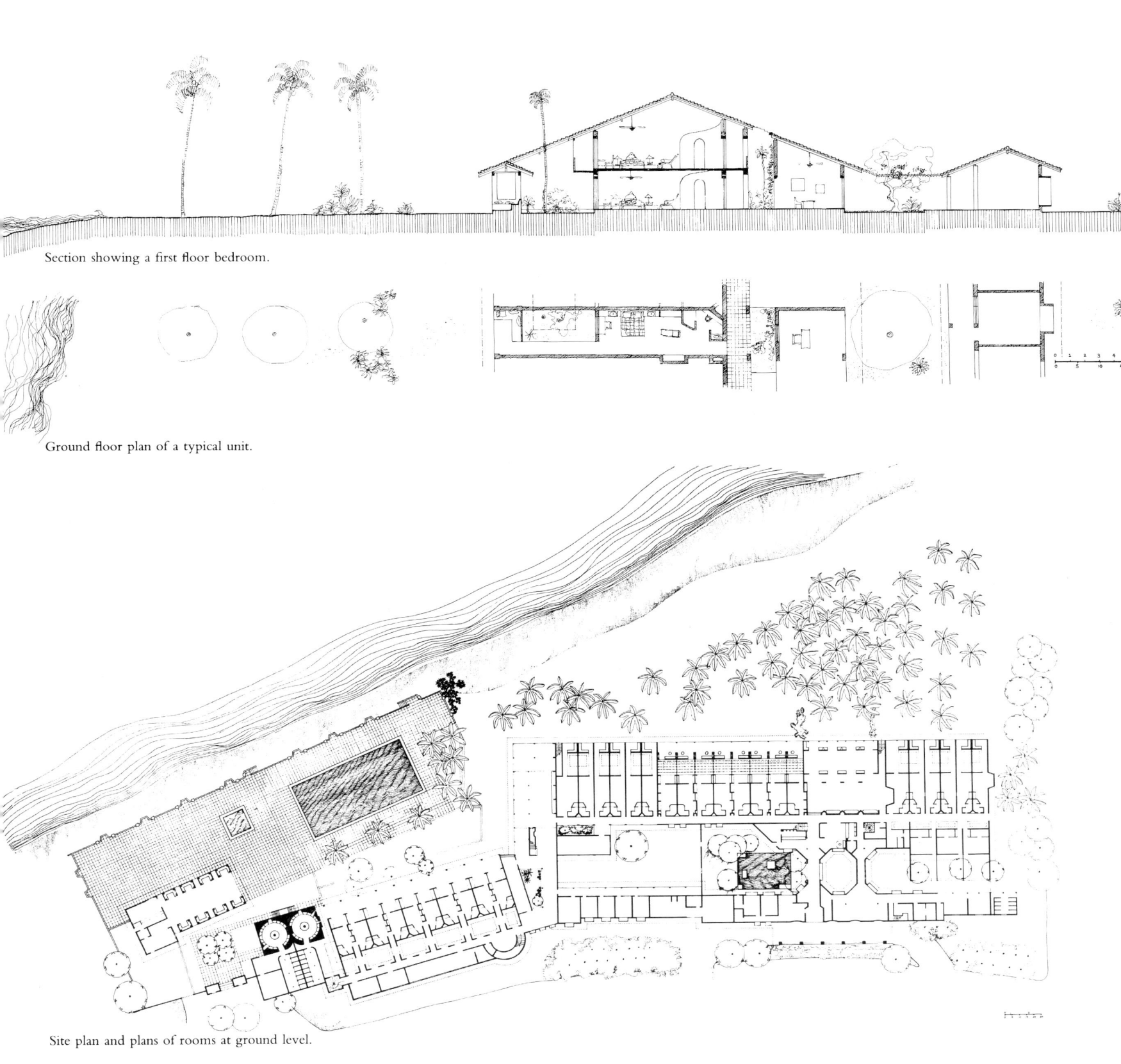

SERENDIB HOTEL

Section showing a first floor bedroom.

Ground floor plan of a typical unit.

Site plan and plans of rooms at ground level.

HOTELS

Snarled Temple trees and pool in the entrance courtyard.

Sail shades on the lawn facing the beach.

View from a ground level bedroom.

PUBLIC BUILDINGS

CEYLON PAVILION EXPO 1970, OSAKA

MADURAI CLUB, SOUTHERN INDIA

SEEMA MALAKA, COLOMBO

NEW PARLIAMENTARY COMPLEX,
SRI JAYAWARDENEPURA, KOTTE

CEYLON PAVILION EXPO 1970, OSAKA

The small pavilion consisted of two glass walled, steel-framed cubes set at an obtuse angle and connected at balcony level. The glass was partly obscured by cut-out paper to prevent glare. Exhibits in the entrance cube, and on the balcony were temple sculptures and gems. In the exit cube visitors could buy Ceylon tea. Paintwork, pedestals and balcony-fronts were white, but both interiors were enriched by the strong colours of banners of modern Ceylonese batik work hung from the ceiling. The dark silhouette seen in the exterior view was a bronzed surface sculpture based on the leaf of the sacred Bo-tree.

The pavilion was notable for austerity and elegance, achieved through economical means harmoniously combined. It was all white and accommodated a few splendid sculptures from Anuradhatura and gold Buddha figurines. Although small the pavilion gave a peculiar sense of spaciousness and tranquility. There was practically no text nor catchword whatsoever.

Exterior facade of the pavilion with the Bo leaf sculpture.

CEYLON PAVILION

Drawing of a tea box for Ceylon tea folded out.

Interior view with banners.

155

MADURAI CLUB, SOUTHERN INDIA

With the acquisition of the premises of the old Madurai Club in the centre of the city, other lands were found; and the new club was built on a more open site shaded by huge banyan trees and overlooking a vista of rice fields and distant mountains. The club building is entirely of granite utilising age old techniques of splitting the stone, providing 12 feet high stone columns and floor paving slabs as big as 10 feet x 5 feet each. The roof structure is of timber beams and posts, while the ceilings are lined with handwoven cotton. All the hardware for doors and windows were hand cast in bronze. A few carved 18th-century columns and antique doors from old demolished houses in the Chettinad district were used in the internal rooms, giving the club its distinctive character.

Stone wall with square window.

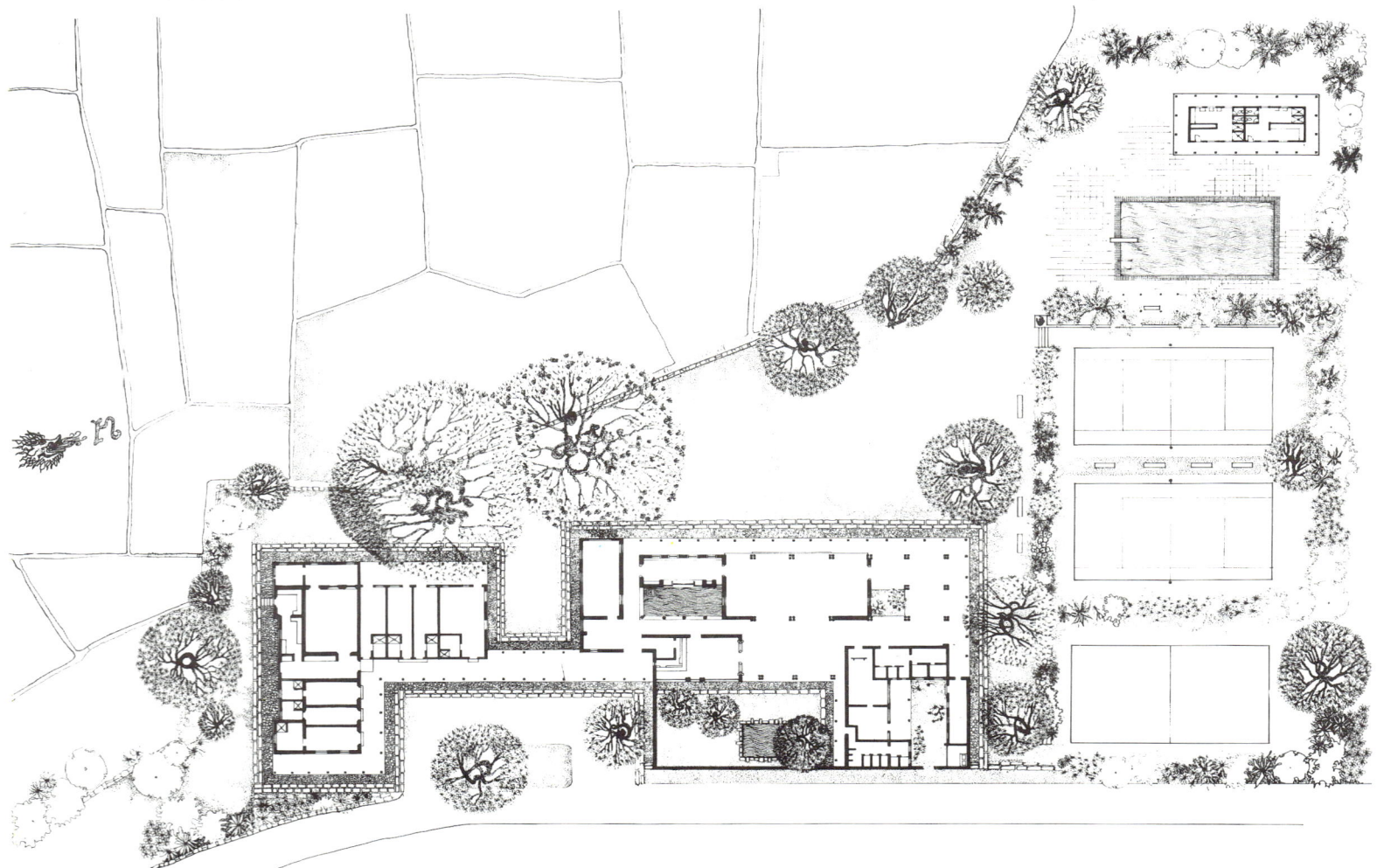

Ground floor plan of club and grounds.

MADURAI CLUB

View of colonnade, glazed screen and the courtyard beyond.

Entrance gallery with cut stone columns.

PUBLIC BUILDINGS

Transversal section.

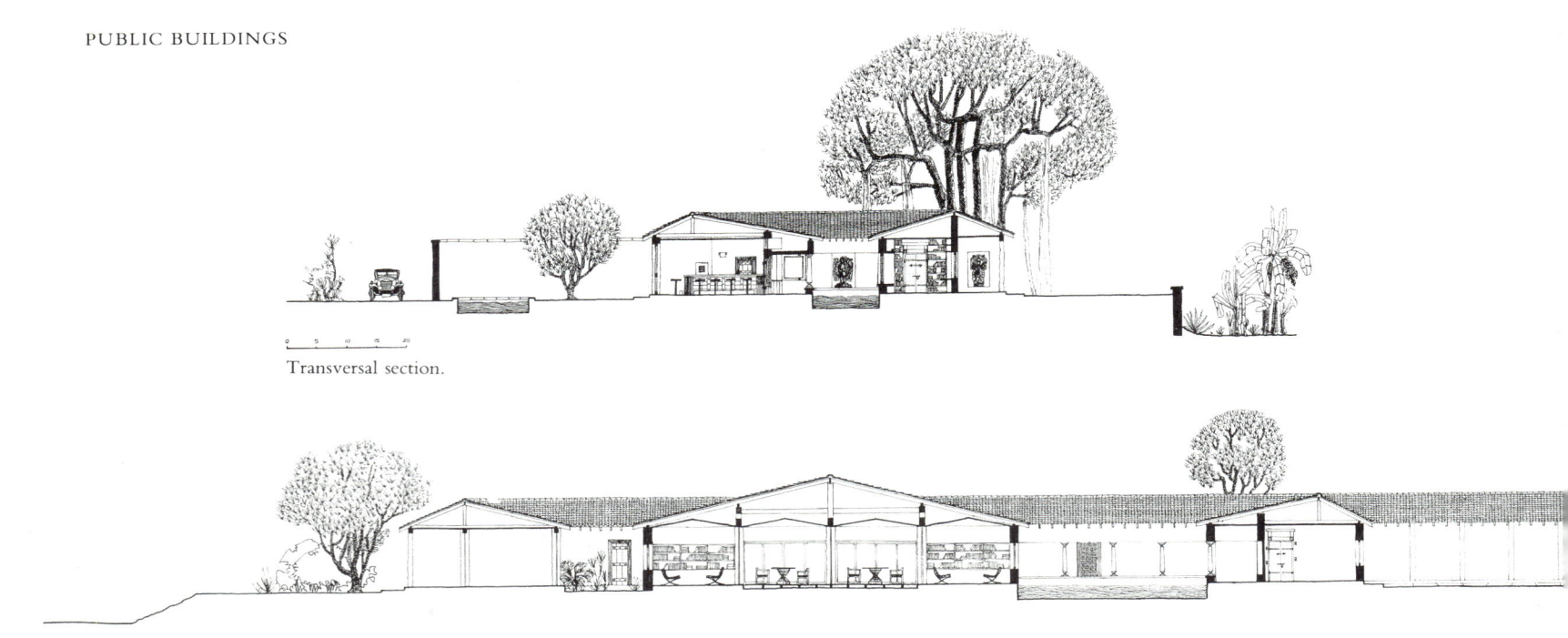

Longitudinal section.

View of a Chettinad door.

Bar viewed from the exterior.

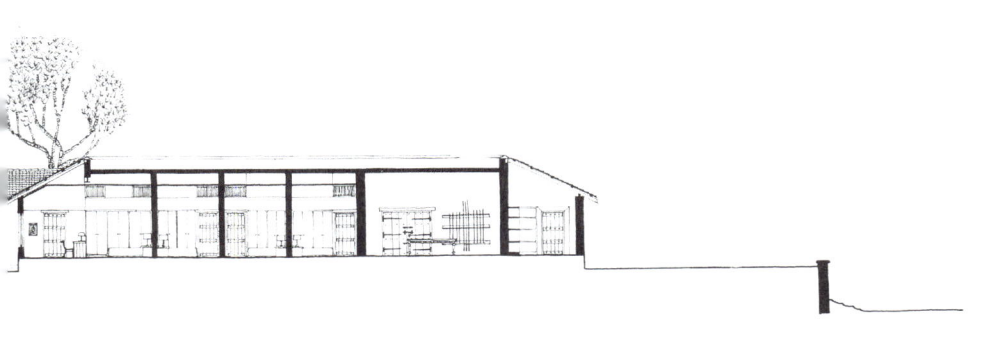

Interior view of the library.

Roof detail of open colonnaded gallery.

View of the gallery with 12-foot-high columns.

MADURAI CLUB

Corner of the club looking towards tennis courts.

View of the pool, the 18th century carved columns and fountain.

Corridor alongside the pool located inside the club.

SEEMA MALAKA, COLOMBO

Three island podiums built on the Beira Lake to serve the nearby Hunupitiya Buddhist Temple. The central pavilion is the chapter house where priests are ordained. The two flanking podiums have on one the sacred Bo tree, and on the other a shrine room.

Overall view of the temple.

End pavilion of the temple.

SEEMA MALAKA

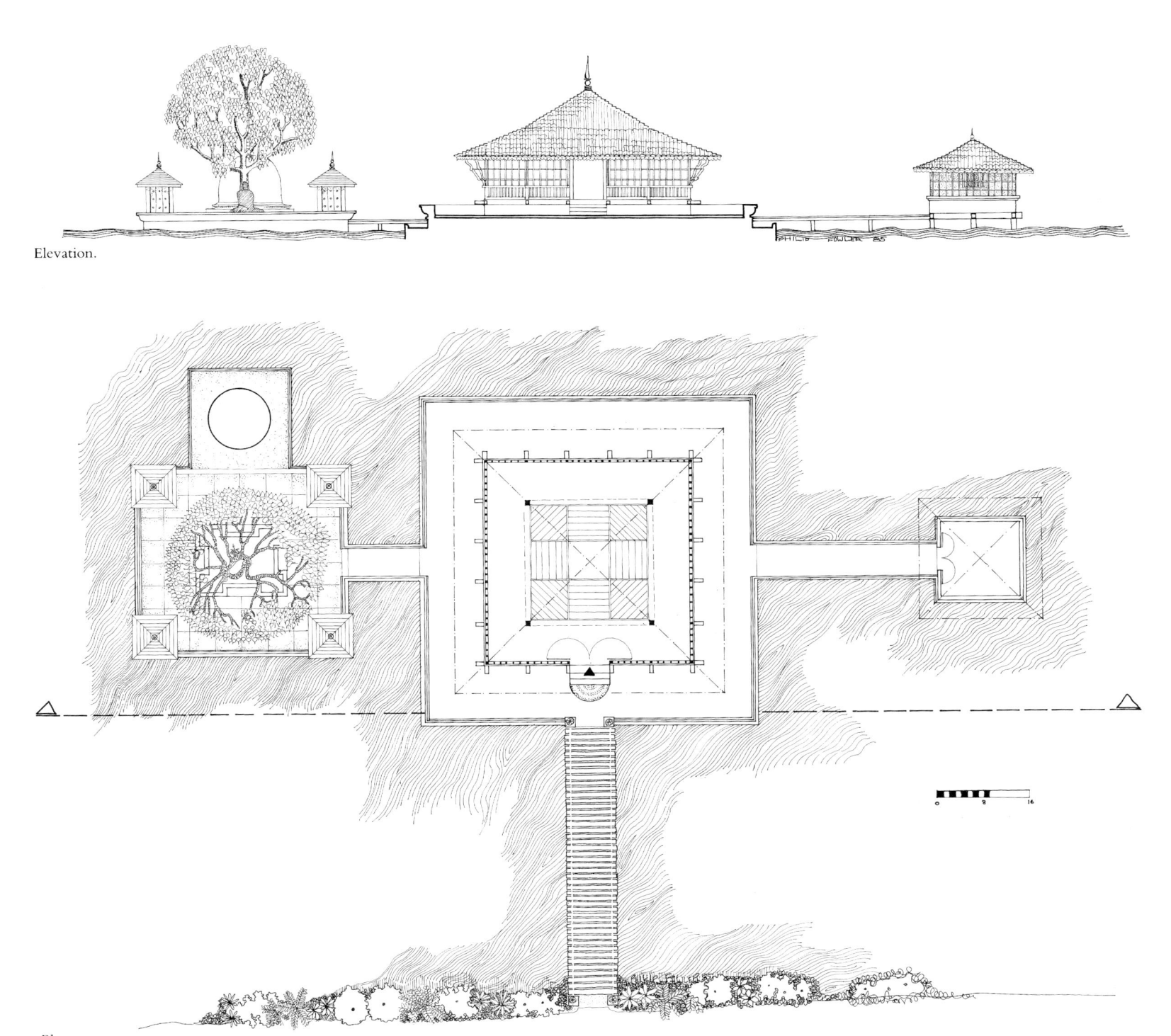

Elevation.

Plan.

NEW PARLIAMENTARY COMPLEX, SRI JAYAWARDENEPURA, KOTTE

When the elections of 1977 brought the present Government into power, one of its first decisions was to build a new Parliament. This had also been considered necessary by previous Governments and plans had been made by government architects for a site in the middle of Colombo. That decision was changed and Kotte — an undeveloped area in the environs of Colombo which had been an important city in the immediate pre-colonial era — was chosen as the new capital city of Sri Lanka: the New Parliament building was now to be sited there.

The site chosen was a marsh around a small island. The marsh was dredged to form a large man-made lake with a wide shore, later to be thickly wooded with indigenous trees. The new Parliament buildings now stand on this island and the approach is across a great causeway and forecourt to the bronze doors in the entrance arcade. Then up the ceremonial stairs leading through the silver doors to the central core of power — the Chamber — within the main pavilion. This main pavilion, with its balconies and galleries, rises three storeys above the two levels of tiered terraces within which are the administrative offices and committee rooms. Other pavilions of varying sizes and functions form part of the main composition of roofs and terraces.

The huge copper roofs of the pavilions, large and small, supported by the traditional patterns of timber and stone columns, have an echo of the monastic and royal buildings of the distant past — yet cover a disposition of spaces which conform to the requirements of an elaborate and careful brief drawn up by a committee of Parliamentarians and administrative officers.

The entire project was completed in the extremely short time of approximately three years from the initial sketch to the opening of this Parliament by the President.

Aerial view of the complex on its island site.

NEW PARLIAMENTARY COMPLEX

Section through the Parliament Chamber.

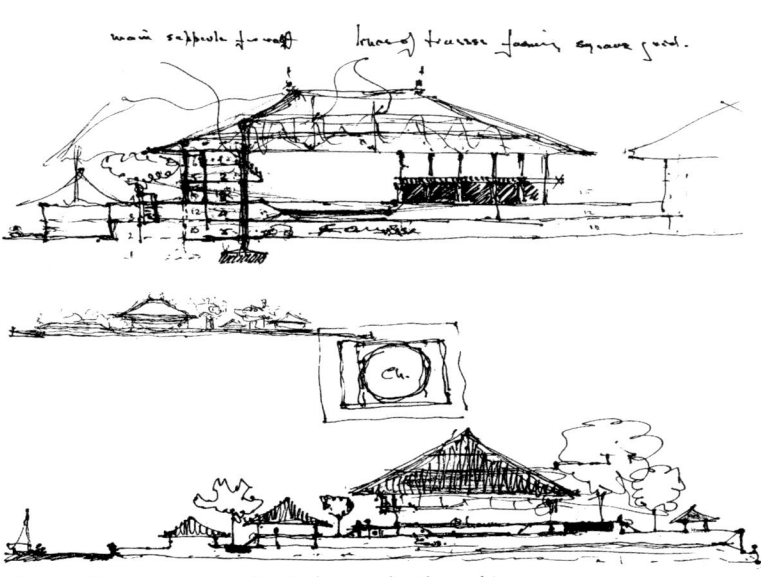

Floor plan at Chamber level.

Early preliminary sketches for Parliament by the architect.

Overleaf: View of the complex.

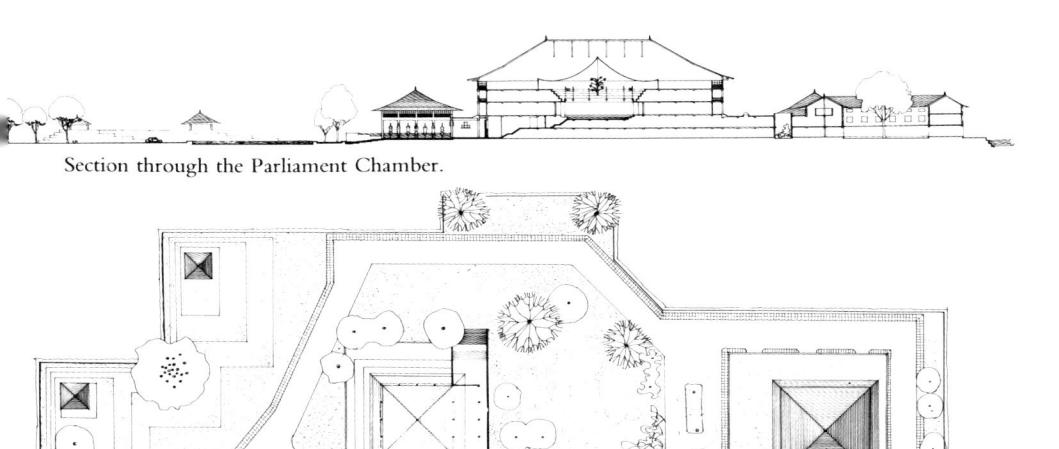

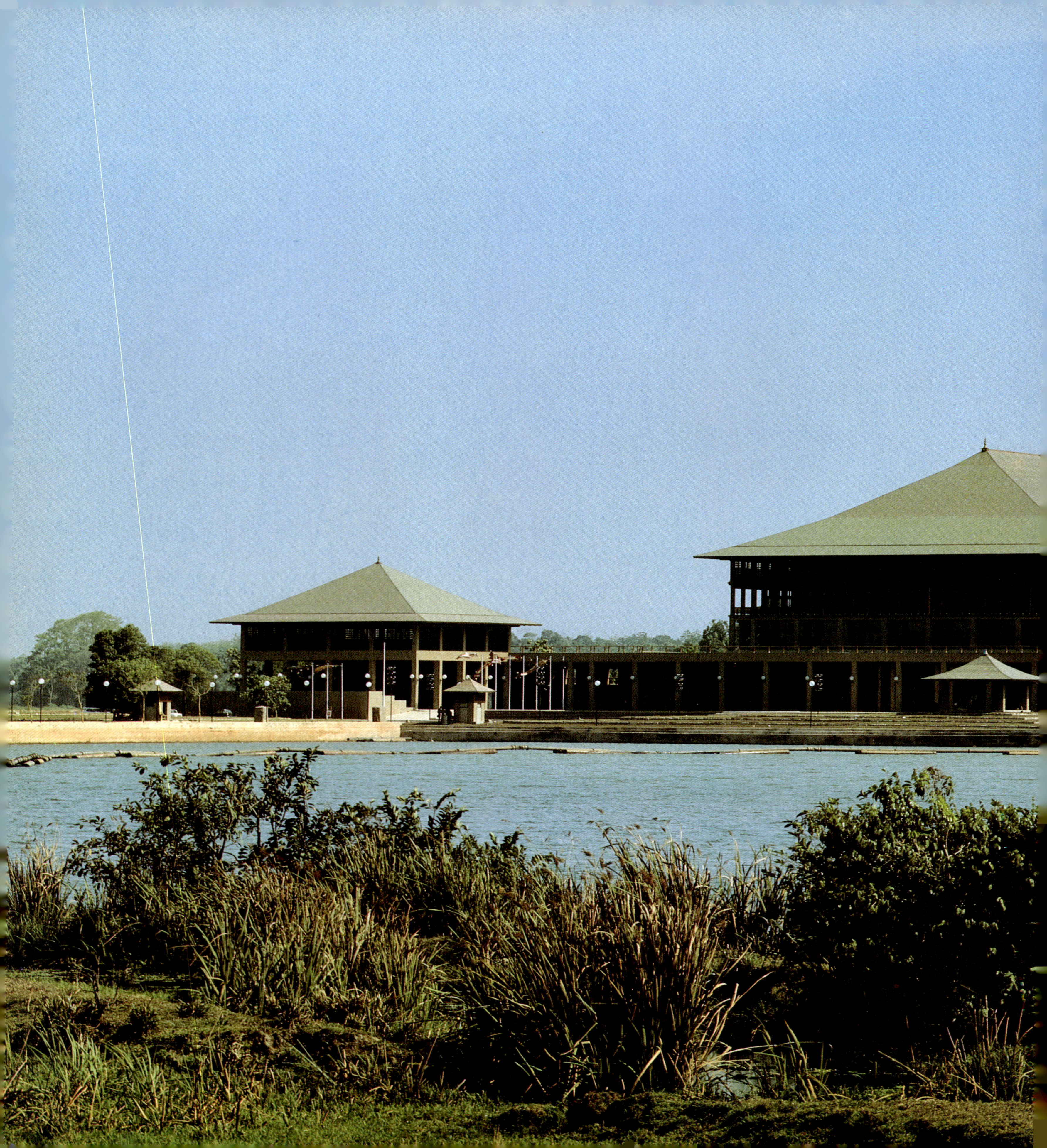

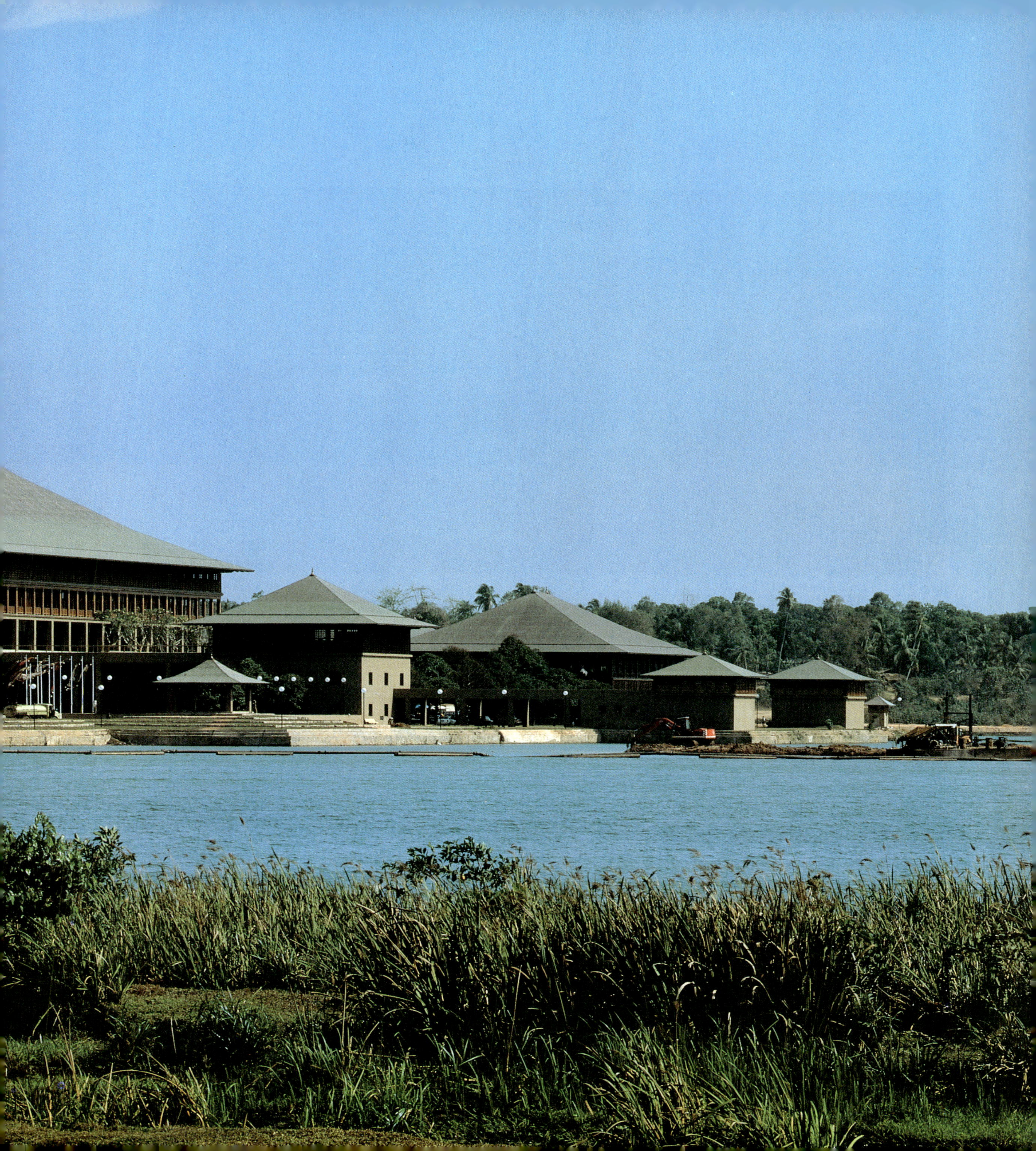

PUBLIC BUILDINGS

Banners in front of the main building.

Detail of the main facade of Parliament pavilion.

View from the upper balcony outside the Parliament Chamber.

Entrance steps with mural decoration.

Main ceremonial entry with bronze doors.
Right: Interior of Parliament Chamber.

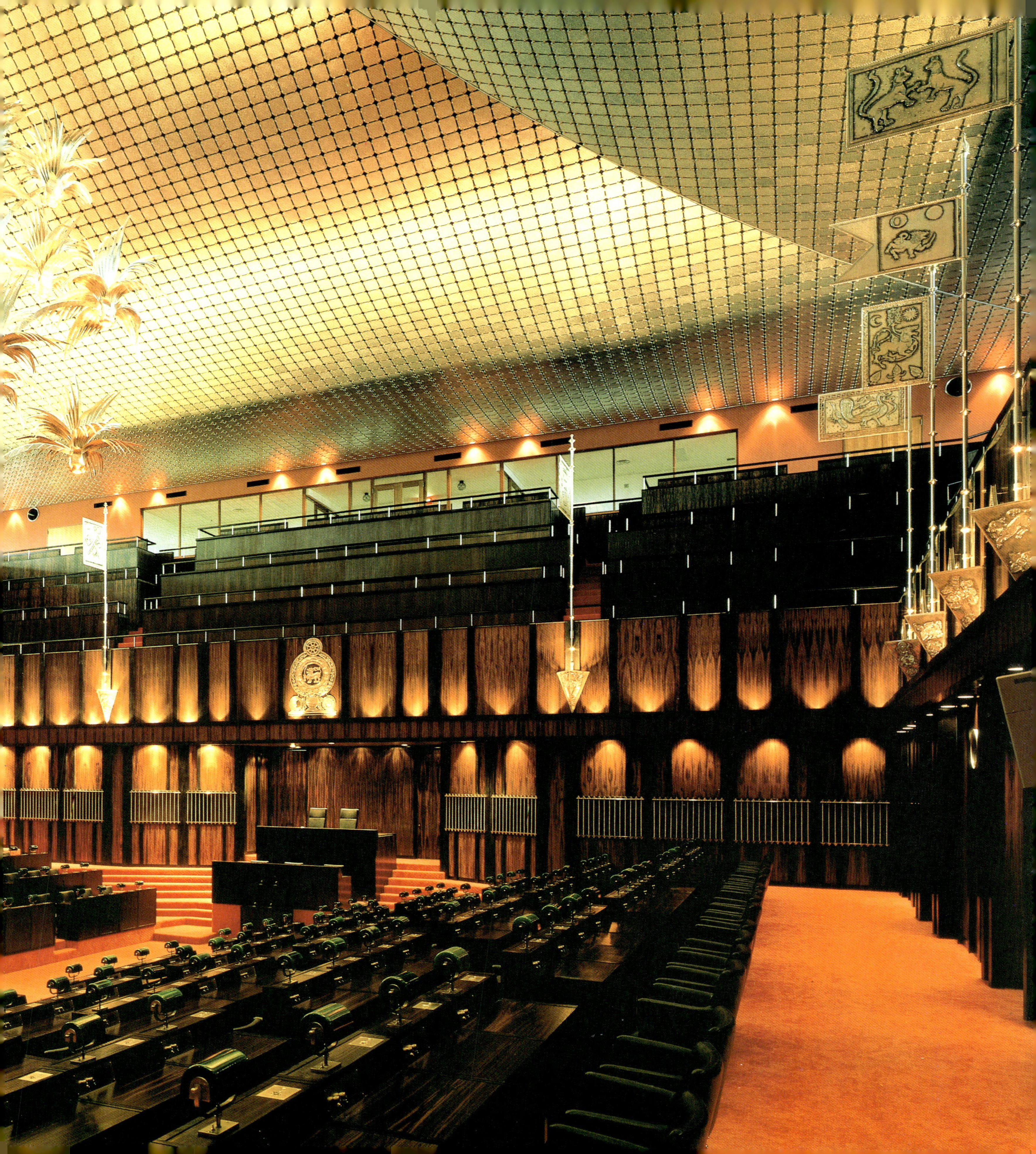

Tunnelled entrance way into reception hall, Kandalama Hotel, Dambulla.

RECENT WORK

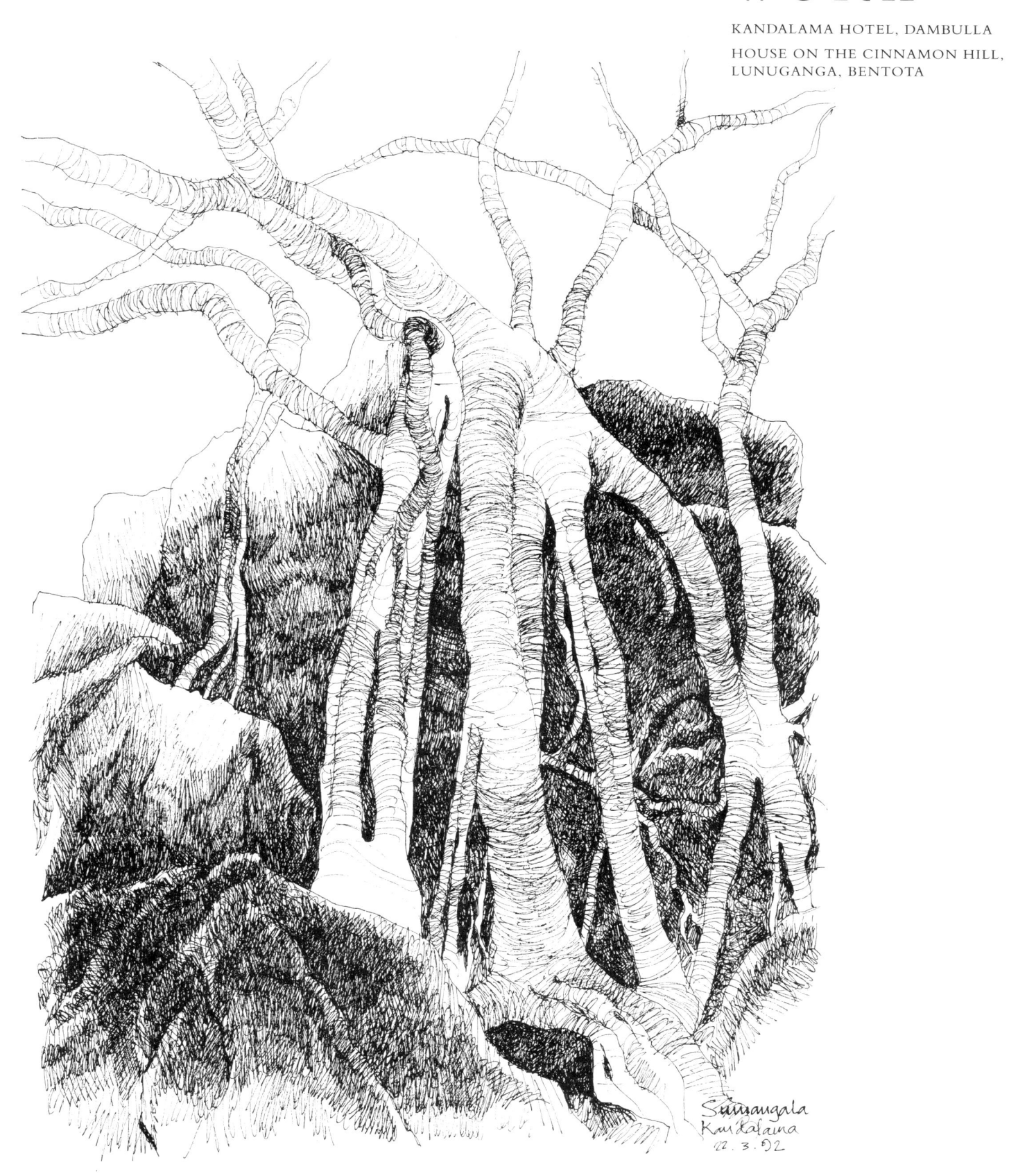

KANDALAMA HOTEL, DAMBULLA

HOUSE ON THE CINNAMON HILL, LUNUGANGA, BENTOTA

KANDALAMA HOTEL, DAMBULLA

On a site first seen from the bund of a third-century lake and then from the air, the hotel was conceived as a belvedere on a series of magic views, as an enjoyment in itself.

Ramp up to entrance and reception verandah

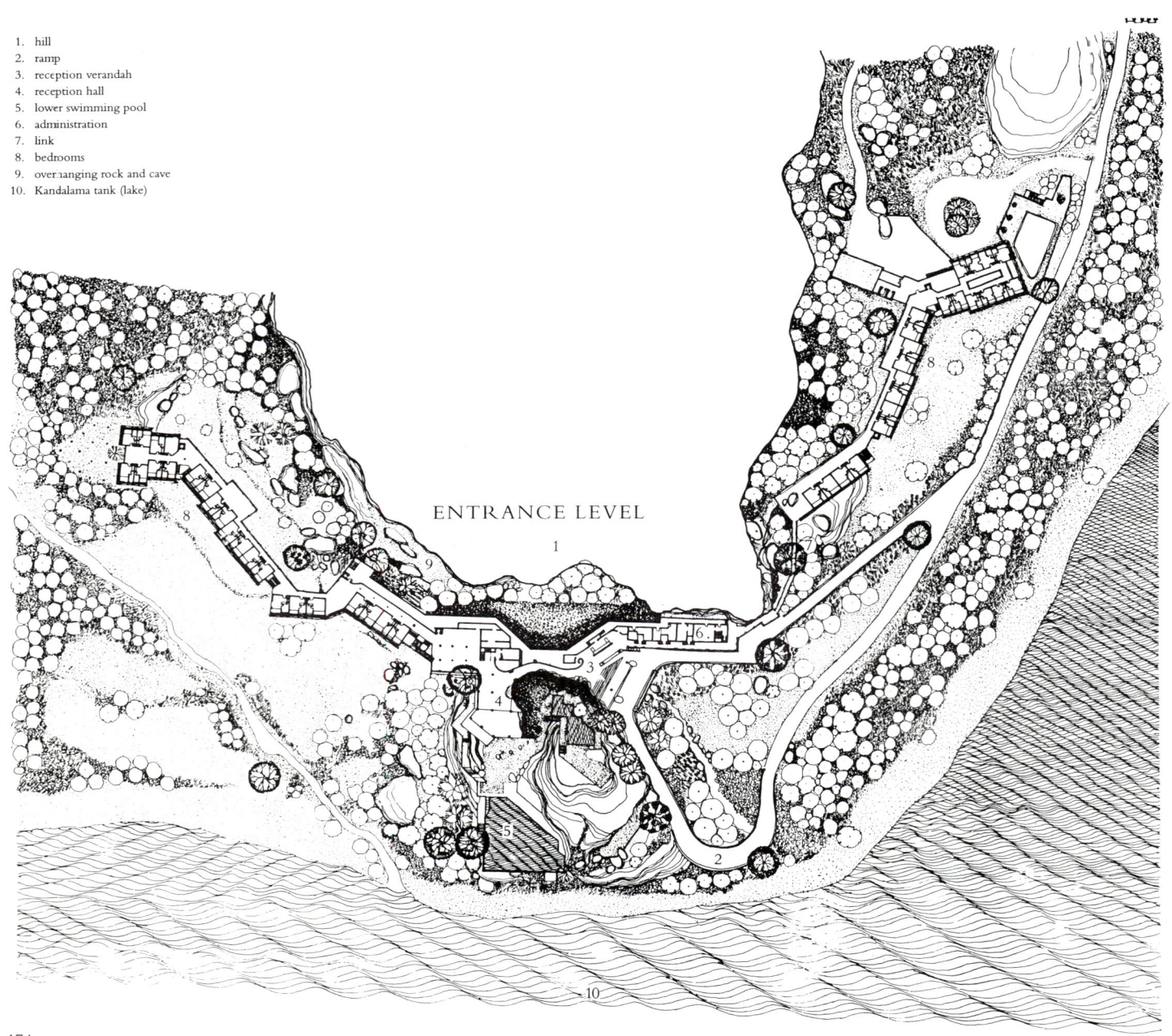

1. hill
2. ramp
3. reception verandah
4. reception hall
5. lower swimming pool
6. administration
7. link
8. bedrooms
9. overhanging rock and cave
10. Kandalama tank (lake)

1. dining room
2. kitchen
3. bar
4. top level swimming-pool
5. overhanging rock and cave
6. restaurant
7. lounge
8. kitchen
9. suite rooms
10. roof terraces
11. library

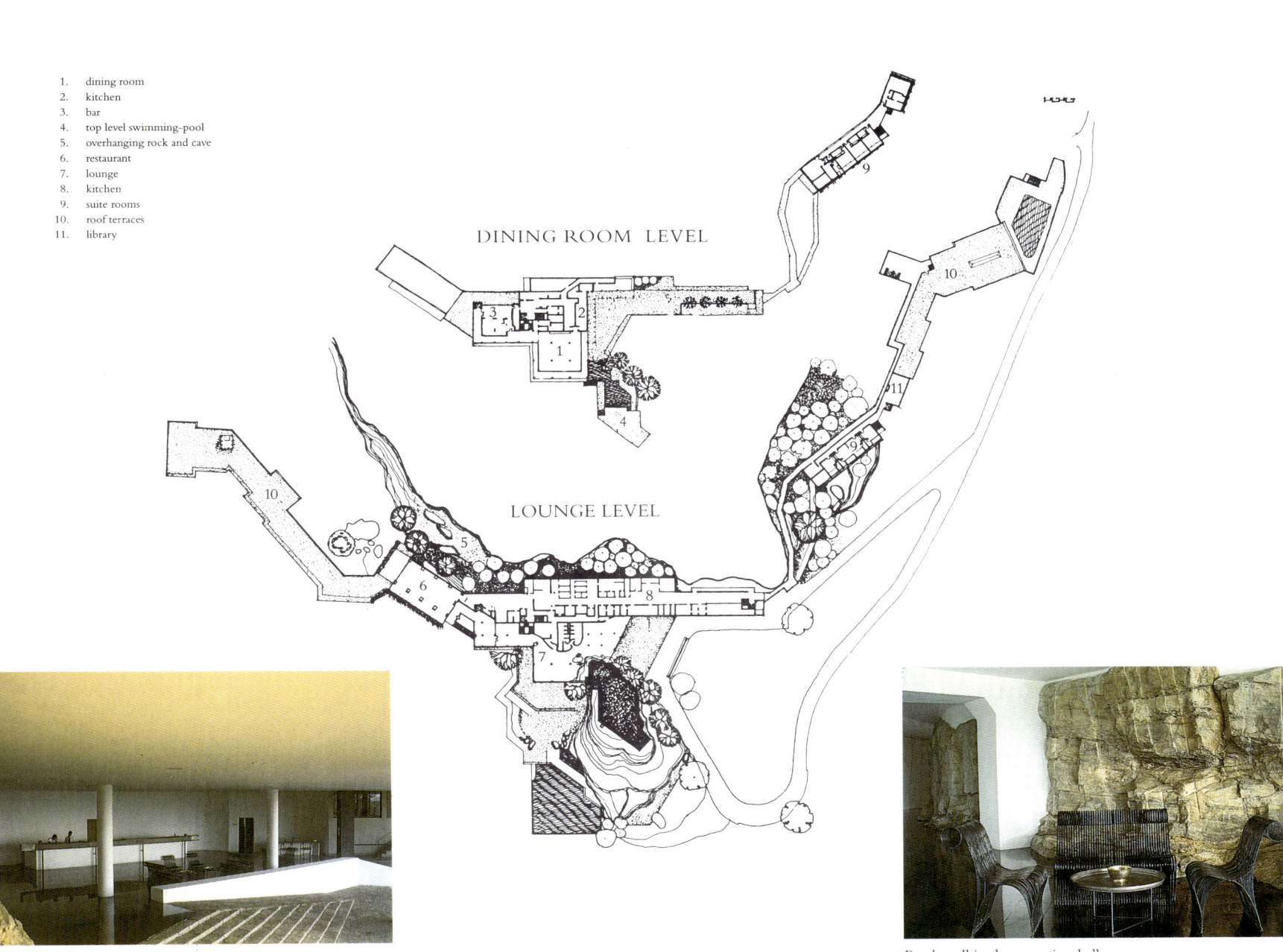

DINING ROOM LEVEL

LOUNGE LEVEL

The reception verandah.

Rock wall in the reception hall.

Owl sculpture by Laki Senanayake in main stair hall.

Pool terraces overlooking Kandalama tank.

Facade of bedroom wing.

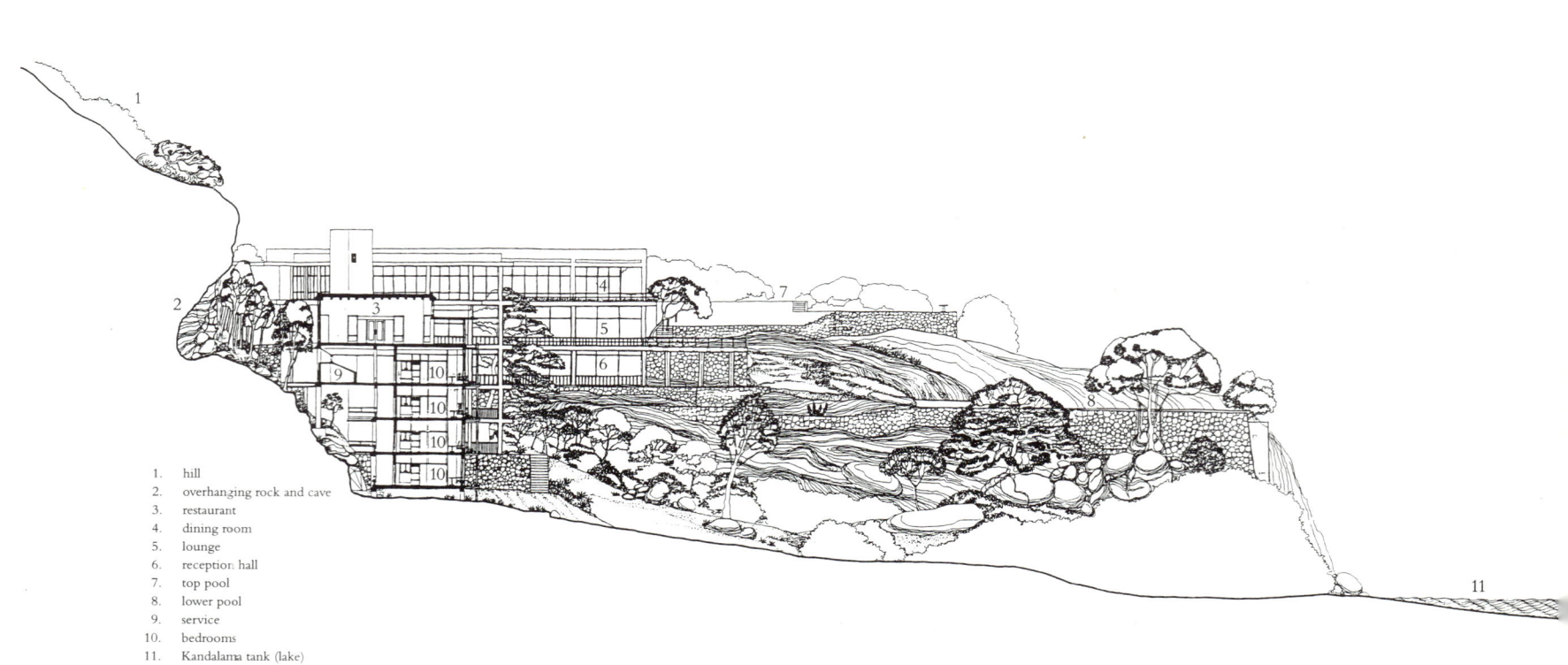

1. hill
2. overhanging rock and cave
3. restaurant
4. dining room
5. lounge
6. reception hall
7. top pool
8. lower pool
9. service
10. bedrooms
11. Kandalama tank (lake)

KANDALAMA HOTEL, DAMBULLA

The hotel from across the lower pool.

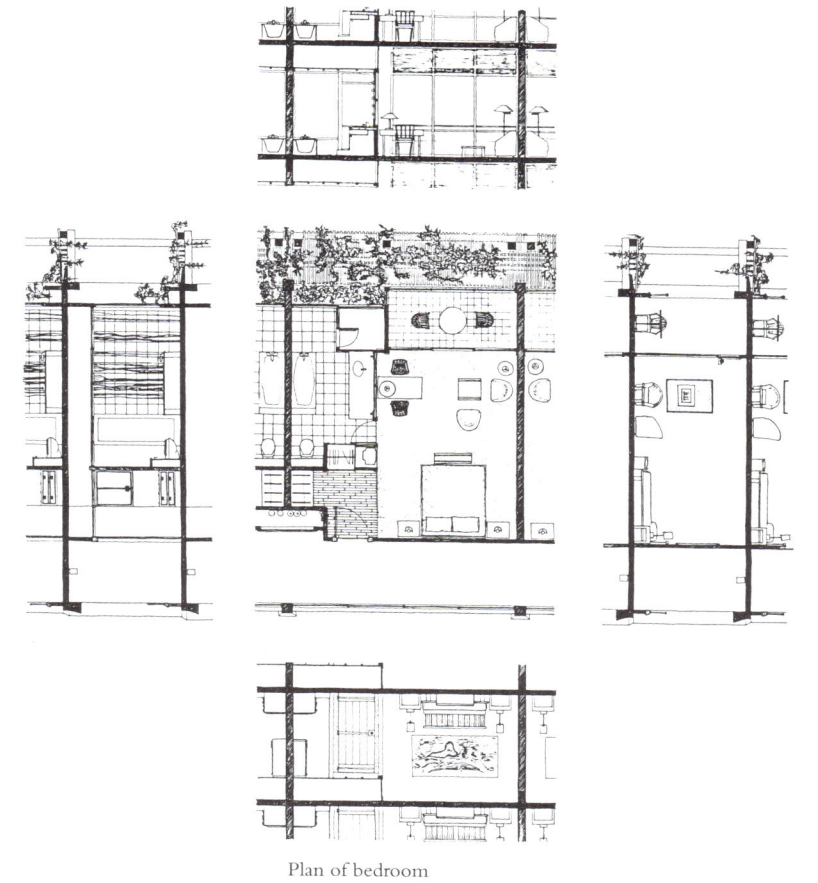

Plan of bedroom

The hotel from reception hall.

HOUSE ON THE CINNAMON HILL, LUNUGANGA, BENTOTA

The initial idea — for a small retreat for contemplation or a studio to be used by a variety of rather different people — has kept this house to an austere and minimal play of space, light and texture, using the basic materials of building. The whole spirit of the house was generated by the views from the southern part of the garden at Lunuganga.

The entrance door approached through a glade.

Exterior of guest room.

Guest room.

Plan

The lake from the loggia at sunrise.

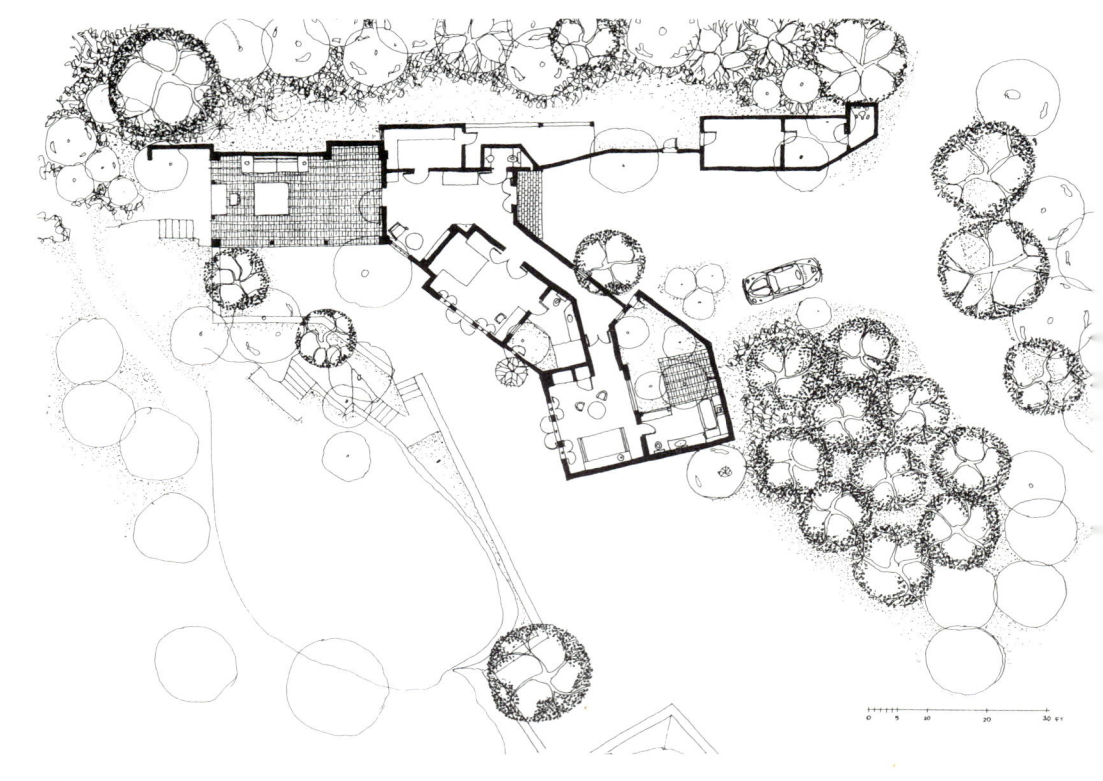

The loggia.

South lawn seen through the loggia.

Bedroom.

Courtyard bathroom.

A BACKGROUND TO GEOFFREY BAWA

Barbara Sansoni

Arguably, Geoffrey Bawa's architecture has a meaning for a Sri Lankan far and beyond any it might have to a foreigner. To Sri Lankans it represents the distallation of centuries of shared experience, and links, at the first level of achievement, its ancient architecture to that of the modern world.

To understand this quality it is necessary to consider, for a moment, the uniqueness of the position of the tiny island of Sri Lanka, anciently Seilon or Ceylon — as it appears in early Arab and the first European texts. This small island off the southern tip of south India, has an extraordinarily rich history for such a small domain. It received Buddhism from Nepal three centuries before Christ and the two beautiful cities of Anaradapura and Polonnaruwa, sculptural and simple, with minimal decoration, are still today its people's pride and inspiration. Its civilisation in the widest sense did not begin with Buddhism nor was it confined to an internal, cultural, spontaneous conclusion. Because of its quite astonishingly important geographical position, the last port of call between East Africa and the Arabian Sea on the one hand and the Bay of Bengal and the Straits of Malacca on the other, all trade by sea between East and West called for water and later to exchange cargo, first in the entreport of Manner and later in Galle and finally Colombo.

It is fascinating and illuminating when thinking of the background of Lanka to remember a few very basic historical dates which contribute to making up the background of every Ceylonese. By 2000 BC there came from the oldest known civilisation — the cities of Mesopotamia — trade and written history to India through the Indus Valley civilisation.

When, in the middle of the first Millenium BC, the centre of power shifted to the mountains of Persia, the Persian Empire extended into Central Asia and right over to Greece, i.e. lands from the Indus to the Aegean were included in one empire. Besides influence from this Indo-Persian Empire, Sri Lanka experienced invaders and settlers from Arabia, southern India, Indonesia and even Melanesia.

After Alexander the Great conquered the Persian Empire in 330 BC, whatever happened to the client states at one end of the Hellenistic Empire in the Ganges Valley, might have been known at the other end of the Greek world, France and Spain. It is a sobering thought that this might have led to the teachings of the Lord Buddha, who died in the preceding century, reaching the Mediterranean, and Greek science and philosophy reaching Southern Asia.

Lanka, small as it was in size but important in its situation as a port, was now in a position to trade between the centre of civilisation, Hellenistic/Roman in the West and Indonesia and China in the East. Trade thereafter rapidly increased in the Indian Ocean, carried especially by Indians from the West coast of India who exchanged goods at the great entreport situated in the area just north of Manner. There they were trans-shipped to Egypt, or possibly to Yemen to avoid the pirates of the Red Sea, whence they went by camel to Alexandria.

At the beginning of the first century AD, the Romans learnt how to sail to Lanka themselves and a Roman Captain wrote 'The Periplus of the Erythrean Sea' or the 'Navigator's Guide to the Indian Ocean' which includes a description of Lanka. Thereafter there is much evidence of a direct Roman prescence in South Asia; Roman houses were found in Pondicherry, East India, less than 200 miles north of Lanka, by Sir Mortimer Wheeler!

By the ninth century AD, Arab ships and crews were sailing, trading and making settlements along the coasts of all South Asia and South East Asia to China. The Muslem Arabs were trading and also converting as they went their way; Malaya, Indonesia, the Maldive Islands are today mostly Islamic. The Moors were in the Iberian peninsular from the eighth to the fifteenth centuries — during the period when they were the most highly civilised community of the Western world, and the most advanced in all the sciences.

When Vasco de Gama rounded the Cape of Good Hope at the end of the fifteenth century and arrived in India he must have found much that was already familiar to him — in much the same way as a Ceylonese today, arriving in north Portugal at Orporto and moving into a hilly landscape divided by river beds in valleys of boulders and rocks, agricultural hill terracing, narrow winding roads and a sandy coast not far away, suffers a confusion of places — a sense of *déjà vu* brought about by the sight of pitched, tiled roofs, grain stores, verandahs, clay finials (can they be Buddhist?) and even small churches with baroque gabled fronts. Here there are town houses arcaded with arches, under which vendors trade; there are carvings on doors and fronts of mediaeval churches which seem to have Hindu excesses; and on the ramparts of frontier towns Portugal and old Ceylon become one.

The roots of this architecture were Hellenistic and the pollinating bees of cross cultural influence were Muslems. The parallels to South Asia are strong.

The Portuguese, who built many of the forts in Ceylon — though some were completed and used by the Dutch — are still remembered for their fine churches and houses with Roman tile roofs, their legacy of courtyards, loggias and verandahs, and for the tradition of fine, turned furniture and carved architectural devices which they adored, for the introduction of Catholicism (as against the old Thomas or Syro Malalbar Christianity) and for their names, so freely adopted by the coastal Singhalse.

The Dutch East India Company, which took over the Portuguese possessions and traded in spices, silks and calico from China to India and Europe by sea continued the cross-pollination of the Arab ships and traders before them. But they were still trading with Islam which was now the main religion of Malaya and Indonesia and also of much of north-west India since the Moghul invasion in the sixteenth century. Colombo had been a Muslim settlement before the Portuguese, and so was Galle outside the Fort and Weligama and Beruwela. In the Kandyan kingdom, Muslims from Sanaa and the Hadramat in Yemen had been totally assimilated into traditional Kandyan society by the King.

Ceylon was ceded to the British by Holland in a treaty of 1796 and a large number of members and employees of the Dutch East India Company, who were not only Dutch but also French, German and Italian, remained as settlers — sometimes planting and farming on estates north of Colombo.

The more sophisticated English-educated settlers moved from Mutwal and the Pettah to new Colombo and together with their Singhalse, Tamil and Muslim friends formed a circle of city social life, thoughful, cultivated, concerned and with enough leisure to be scholarly and sporting and often both. They had careers in many branches of island life — the judiciary, the Ceylon Civil Service, medicine, education, liberal-minded men firmly linked in friendship, widely and deeply read, well informed and well connected, one can see now why and how these Ceylonese of widely differing racial origins contributed to the making up of the term "Ceylonese" from its earliest history and were able to adapt with tremendous style and humorous balance — because they had a long history of adapting and being accustomed to outside influence and change. It was into their world that Geoffrey Bawa was born.

It was a world of absolute security for a child in which everyone knew each other and was connected by close friendship, blood or marriage. Some were rich, some poor, some virtuous, others wicked — the bond was an infinite ability to make allowances, to have unending tolerance, and it was certainly needed as these eccentric families had eccentrics of both the egotistical and idealistic kind of great extreme. Their houses, pillared, verandahed and airy, were filled with furniture, utensils, *objets d'art* and pottery from the long maritime history of our island centred on a trade route.

Geoffrey Bawa read English and Law at Cambridge and having taken his degree spent four to five years travelling to America, Europe and the Far East but it would seem that Italy was the catalyst to his architectural thinking.

When back in Ceylon he became almost totally involved in the pleasures of altering his house and transforming the rubber plantation into a wonderfully beautiful, rolling landscape; staircased and terraced, squared into paddy fields, on the edge of a long lake with a wild island in its centre. This he so enjoyed that he decided to become an architect.

Since then he has been able to express his values, likes and enthusiasms and his many faceted talents in the buildings he not only designed but built, imparting to each one a personal sense of involvement which gives his work a delight which may well stem from his being heir to the many varied cultures of Ceylon. This deep understanding and visual appreciation of past and present appears in all his work and, for myself, sums up our history in an evolving modern architecture — because as I said at the beginning — 'arguably Geoffrey Bawa's architecture has a meaning to a Sri Lankan far and beyond any it might have to a foreigner.' To Sri Lankans it represents the distillation of centuries of shared experience, and links at the first level of achievement, its ancient architecture to that of the modern world'.

CHRONOLOGY OF WORKS

1950
THE GARDEN, LUNUGANGA, Bentota.

1958
PAUL AND PRINI DERANIYAGALA HOUSE, Guildford Crescent, Colombo.

1959
CARMEN GUNASEKERA HOUSE, Colombo.

CLUB HOUSE, Ratnapura.
This simple country tennis club house is on a sloping, well-planted site with large trees. Except for the changing rooms and bar, the whole space was open and all the columns were timber rough-hewn tree-trunks of hard wood set in brass shoes with cast brass capitals. The terraces within the club house stepped down overlooking four tennis courts.

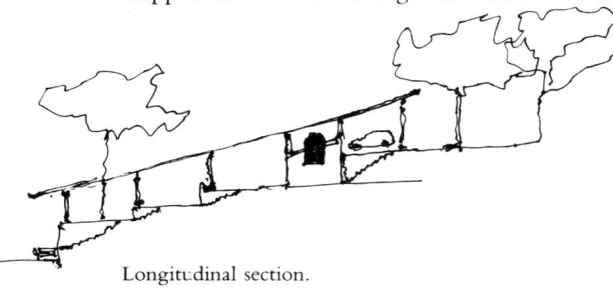

Longitudinal section.

1960
DR. A.S.H. DE SILVA HOUSE, Galle.
House for a doctor in Galle, on a sloping site, with the house in the upper part of the site, with a corridor leading down to the dispensary and surgery by the roadside.

Interior reflecting pool.

MANAGER'S HOUSE, Stratspey Estate, Upcot.

Exterior view.

1961
AELIAN KANNANGARA HOUSE, Horton Place, Colombo.

SHANMUGADASAN HOUSE, Torrington Avenue, Colombo.

WIJEMANNE FLATS, Green Path, Colombo.

SAMMY DIAS BANDARANAIKE FLATS, Rotunda Gardens, Colombo.

1962
ENA DE SILVA HOUSE, Colombo.

1963
CLASSROOM EXTENSION FOR ST. THOMAS' PREPARATORY SCHOOL, Colombo.
Two new classroom blocks were needed on a site by the sea. These were executed entirely in vibrated concrete, with certain elements which were pre-cast, and a giant relief mural by Anil Jayasuriya.

Facade with relief mural facing Galle Road.

PIN AND PAM FERNANDO HOUSE, Alexandra Place, Colombo.
A house in which careful attention was given to every detail, and the best materials used. The gutters and downpipes were of copper. All the timber was of selected Burma teak, and rafter ends were cased in copper. This was the first instance of the sliding window walls being used to give maximum opening to the living room. The Martenstyn Tower, which was built later for the daughter of the house, now encroaches on the tennis courts on the west side of this site.

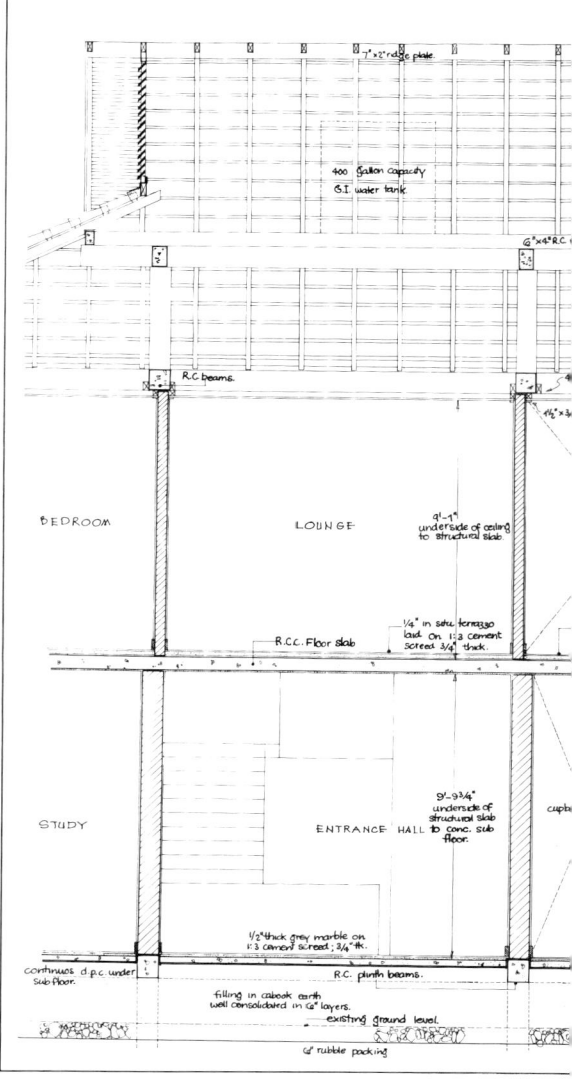

Detailed execution drawing for construction.

THE ARCHITECT'S OFFICE, Colombo.

CLASSROOM EXTENSION FOR BISHOPS' COLLEGE, BOYD PLACE, Colombo.
The ground floor is open for General Assembly, and includes a gold-leaf sculpture of a Manzu Bishop done by Lydia Duccini.

Exterior view.

1964
CHRIS AND CARMEL RAFFEL HOUSE, Ward Place, Colombo.
A house in Colombo was conceived for a doctor whose wife is a musician. The ground floor was planned to allow virtually the whole site to be used for small concerts. As the site was restricted the staircase rose to a central tower with a terrace at the top.

Interior view showing ceiling carpentry work.

UPALI WIJEWARDENE HOUSE, Thurstan Road, Colombo.
Situated against a main road, the client wanted complete privacy, and internal courtyards on each floor of his house. The roof was flat with large plant troughs and pavilions to be used as the main garden space of the house. A reinforced concrete frame structure was used, and to soften the severity of the framed facades, the pavilions on the garden floor had gilded flat ceilings.

Exterior view before more recent additions.

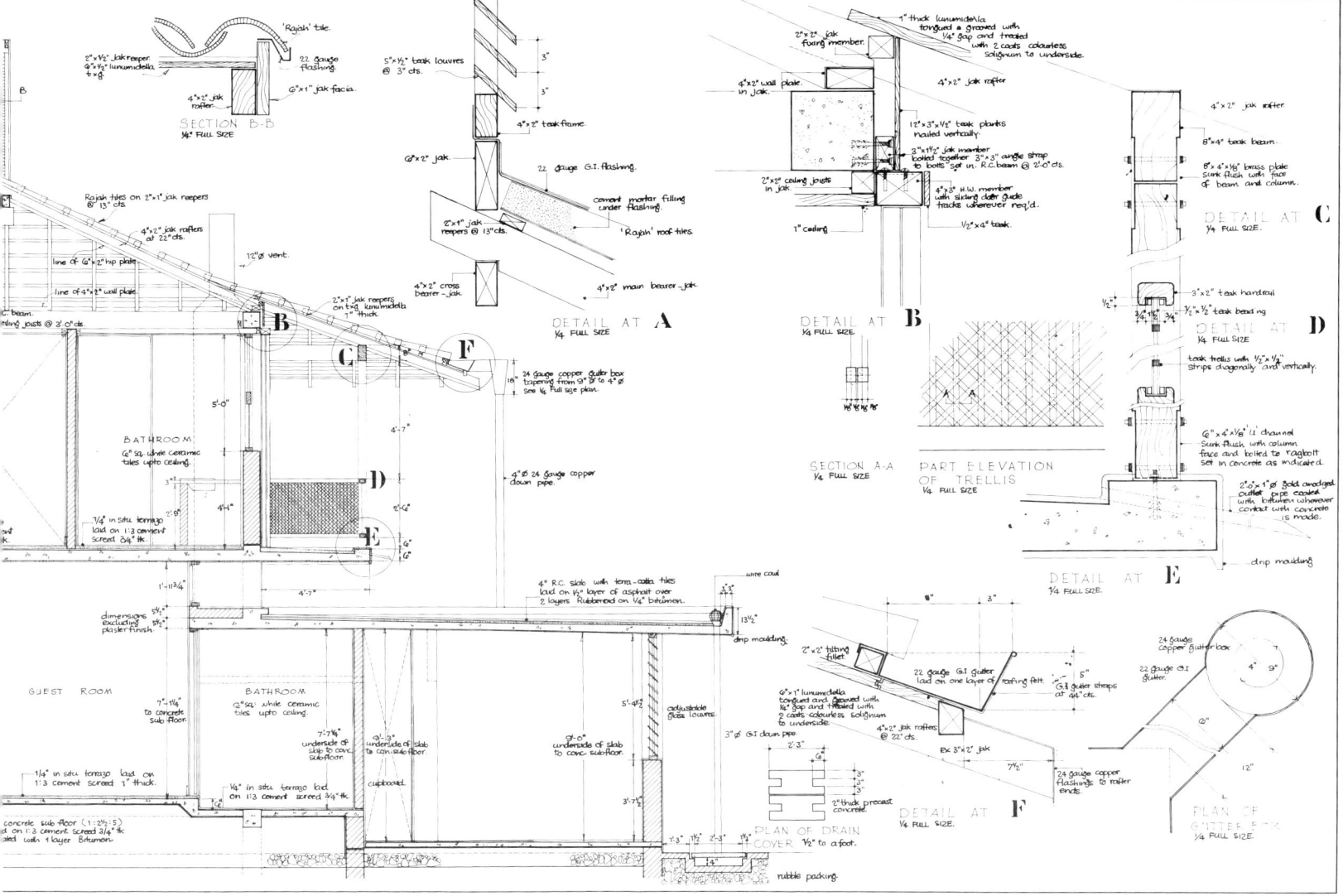

Pin and Pam Fernando House.

LEELA DIAS BANDARANAYAKE HOUSE, Mount Lavinia.

ST. BRIDGET'S MONTESSORI SCHOOL, Colombo.

1966
CHARTERED BANK HOUSES, Queen's Road, Colombo.

CLASSROOM EXTENSION FOR LADIES' COLLEGE, Flower Road, Colombo.

YAHAPATH ENDERA FARM SCHOOL, Hanwella.

ADDITIONS AND RENOVATIONS TO CORAL GARDENS HOTEL, Hikkaduwa, (now demolished). This was the first hotel under the tourist development plan of the Government. An existing resthouse was altered and enlarged. It has now been demolished to make way for a large commercial hotel.

BLUE LAGOON HOTEL, Negombo.

Y.W.C.A., Rotunda Gardens, Colombo.

AIRLINE OFFICE INTERIOR, U.T.A., Prince Street, Colombo (subsequently altered).

1967
ESTATE BUNGALOW, Polontalawa (with Ulrik Plesner).

ESTATE BUNGALOW, Beruwana (designed).

1968
STEEL CORPORATION OFFICES, Oruwela.

1969
THE ARCHITECT'S HOUSE, Colombo.

PIETER KEUNEMAN HOUSE, Inner Flower Road, Colombo.

MAHAHALPE FARM between Kandy and Galaha.
Lying along a steeply sloping ridge with spectacular views, this was to house the first silk-worm farm in Sri Lanka. Built for the congregation of the Good Shepherd nuns.

BENTOTA BEACH HOTEL, Bentota.
Bentota Tourist Complex, Bentota.
In 1966 the Government Tourist Board chose 60 acres on the seacoast of Bentota for the first major tourist development. The Resort and the two hotels — Bentota Beach, and Serendib — were planned within this area. The additions to the two hotels, a complex of buildings such as shops, restaurants, railway stations, police stations were also planned so that these would be in sympathy with the whole development.

1970
CEYLON PAVILION EXPO '70 Osaka, Japan.

PUBLIC LIBRARY, Kalutara.

1971
SERENDIB HOTEL, Bentota.

SCIENCE BLOCK for Vidyodaya Campus, University of Sri Lanka, Nugegoda. The site adjoins an arts faculty, and a new science faculty was planned for this complex. The buildings were carefully related to the slight level changes in the site.

INDUSTRIAL ESTATE, Pallekelle.
Built for the Industrial Development Board, this complex consists of three types of buildings catering for three different categories of small industries. These buildings were roofed with tiles and asbestos, and clad with multiple units of asbestos and glass combinations to suit the requirements of the individual categories.

Exterior view of one building type.

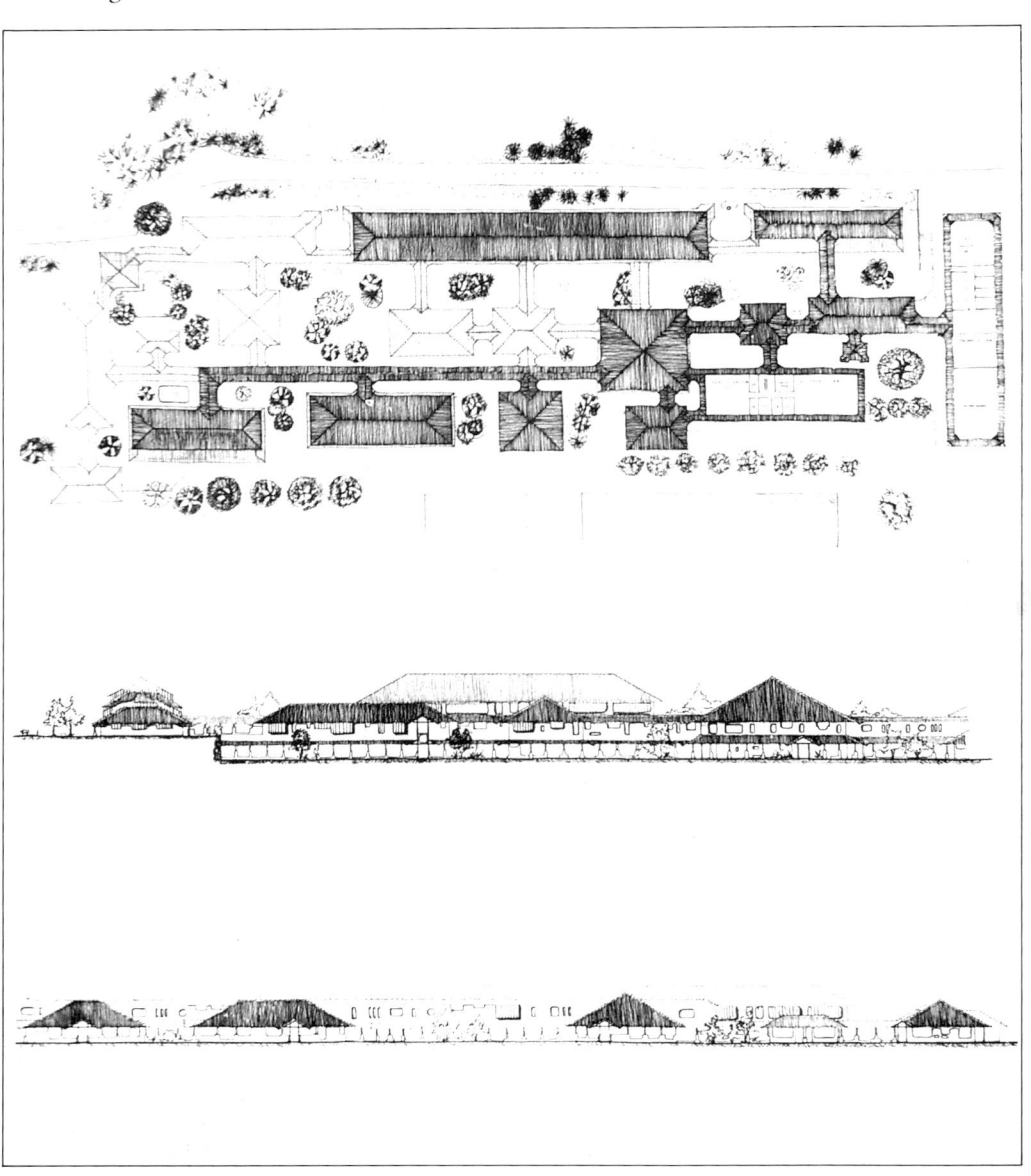

Site plan and elevations. Science Block, Vidyodaya.

1972
STANLEY DE SARAM HOUSE, Colombo.

1973
F.C. DE SARAM TERRACE HOUSES, 5th Lane, Colombo.
An innovation in Colombo housing, these four houses were built as a terrace. Courtyards and gardens were laid to the rear of the site, and only the entrance halls and garages abutted the road. Each house has a separate identity achieved by the use of colour and small differences in detail.

PAVILIONS, Batujimbar, Bali.

1974
PETER WHITE HOUSE, Mauritius.

MADURAI CLUB, Southern India.

NEPTUNE HOTEL, Beruwela.
A medium-cost hotel built on a long narrow site between other hotels so that the planning demanded that the hotel looked in on itself. Nevertheless, all the rooms had a view of the sea, and the landscaping forms a very important part in achieving the dramatic pleasurable qualities required of sea-side hotels.

1975
AGRARIAN RESEARCH AND TRAINING INSTITUTE, Colombo.

1976
HERBERT AND NORMA TENNEKOON HOUSE, 33rd Lane, Colombo.

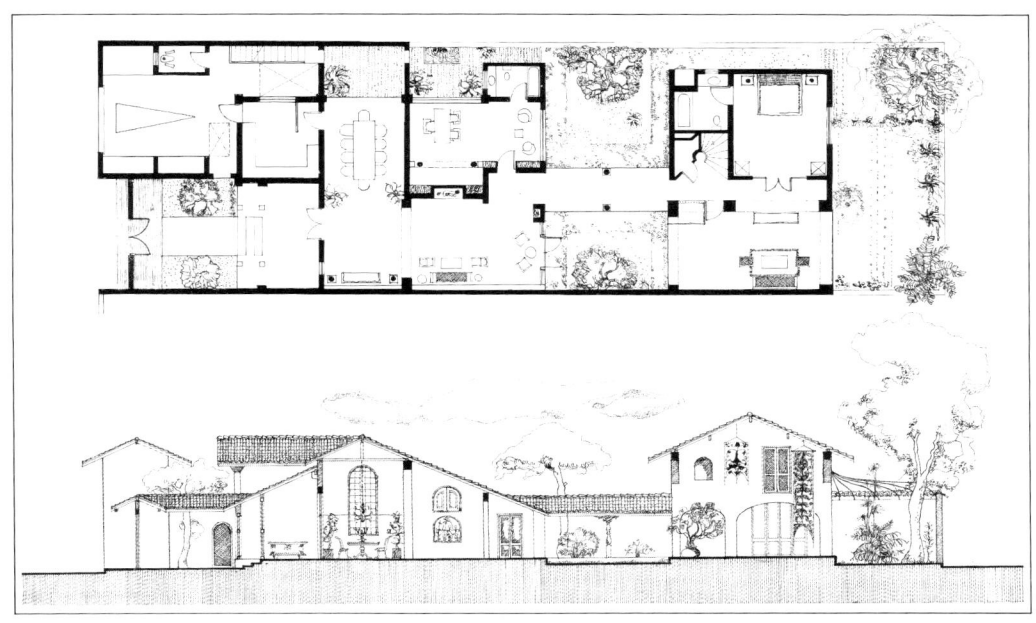

Ground floor plan and section.

Lounge area. Neptune Hotel.

NATIONAL INSTITUTE OF MANAGEMENT, McCarthy Road, Colombo.

HOTEL CONNAMARA RENOVATIONS, India.
A reinforced concrete structural frame with glass and red brick infill was devised for this five-storey building.

1977
CLASSROOM EXTENSION FOR OVERSEAS CHILDRENS' SCHOOL, Muttiah Road, Colombo.

PANAMA HOTEL, Panama (designed).

CANDOLINE HOTEL, Goa (designed).

SEEMA MALAKA; Beira Lake, Colombo.

1978
LIDIA GUNASEKERA HOUSE, Bentota.

ANURA BANDARANAIKE HOUSE, Rosmead Place, Colombo.

MAHAWELI OFFICE BUILDING, Darley Road, Colombo.
The site largely shaped the plan of the building, which was wholly irregular. For natural airflow a cill ventilator was incorporated. The angular nature of its planning, and the open plan of all the office space provides good views and a maximum amount of light and ventilation. Its apparently massive construction is tempered by a remarkable transparency.

MEENA MUTTIAH HOSPITAL FOR THE KUMARANI OF CHETTINAD, Madras (designed).

1979

RATNA SIVARATNAM HOUSE, Bullers Road, Colombo.

EXTENSIONS AND RENOVATIONS TO FRENCH AMBASSADOR'S RESIDENCE, Alfred Place, Colombo.

HAMEED Beach Villa, Bentota.

CLUB VILLA, Bentota.

ADMINISTRATION COMPLEX AND HOUSING FOR FERTILISER CORPORATION, Sapugaskanda.

POLICE STATION FOR NEPTUNE HOTEL, Beruwela.

INTERIOR, INDO SUEZ BANK, Ceylinco Building, Queen Street, Colombo.

1981

MARTENSTYN TOWER, Alexandra Place, Colombo.

On the west side of a garden, close against the house built earlier (see house for Pin and Pam Fernando), accommodation had to be provided for their daughter and yet privacy preserved for the occupants of both the new and the old house.

INTEGRAL EDUCATION CENTRE, Piliyandala.

VOCATIONAL TRAINING INSTITUTE FOR LADIES' COLLEGE, Inner Flower Road, Colombo.

TEACHING CENTRE AND HEADQUARTERS FOR THE BRITISH COUNCIL, Alfred House Gardens, Colombo.

CARGO BOAT DEVELOPMENT CO. LTD., Queen Street, Colombo.

TRITON HOTEL, Ahungalla.

1982

OFFICES FOR H.T.L. THOMPSON (LANKA) LIMITED, Joseph Frazer Road, Colombo.

NEW PARLIAMENTARY COMPLEX, Sri Jayawardenepura, Kotte.

1983

CONVERSION OF OLD PARLIAMENT INTO PRESIDENTIAL SECRETARIAT AND ARCHIVES, Lotus Road, Colombo.

1984

SUNETRA NANAYAKARA HOUSE, Horagolla.

PHASE I: SCIENCE FACULTIES AND STAFF RESIDENCES, Ruhunu University, Matara.

GALADARI HOTEL, Islamabad, Pakistan (designed).

A project was developed for a luxury hotel of 200 rooms on the main avenue opposite the Presidential Palace at Islamabad. It was thought necessary to preserve the feeling of indigenous architecture and the entire hotel in local brick in tones of soft brown. The domes were to be gilded ceramic mosaic, and all the floors of white Pakistan marble. The protected inner spaces of the old caravanserai was achieved in the vast entrance lobby and also in the atrium.

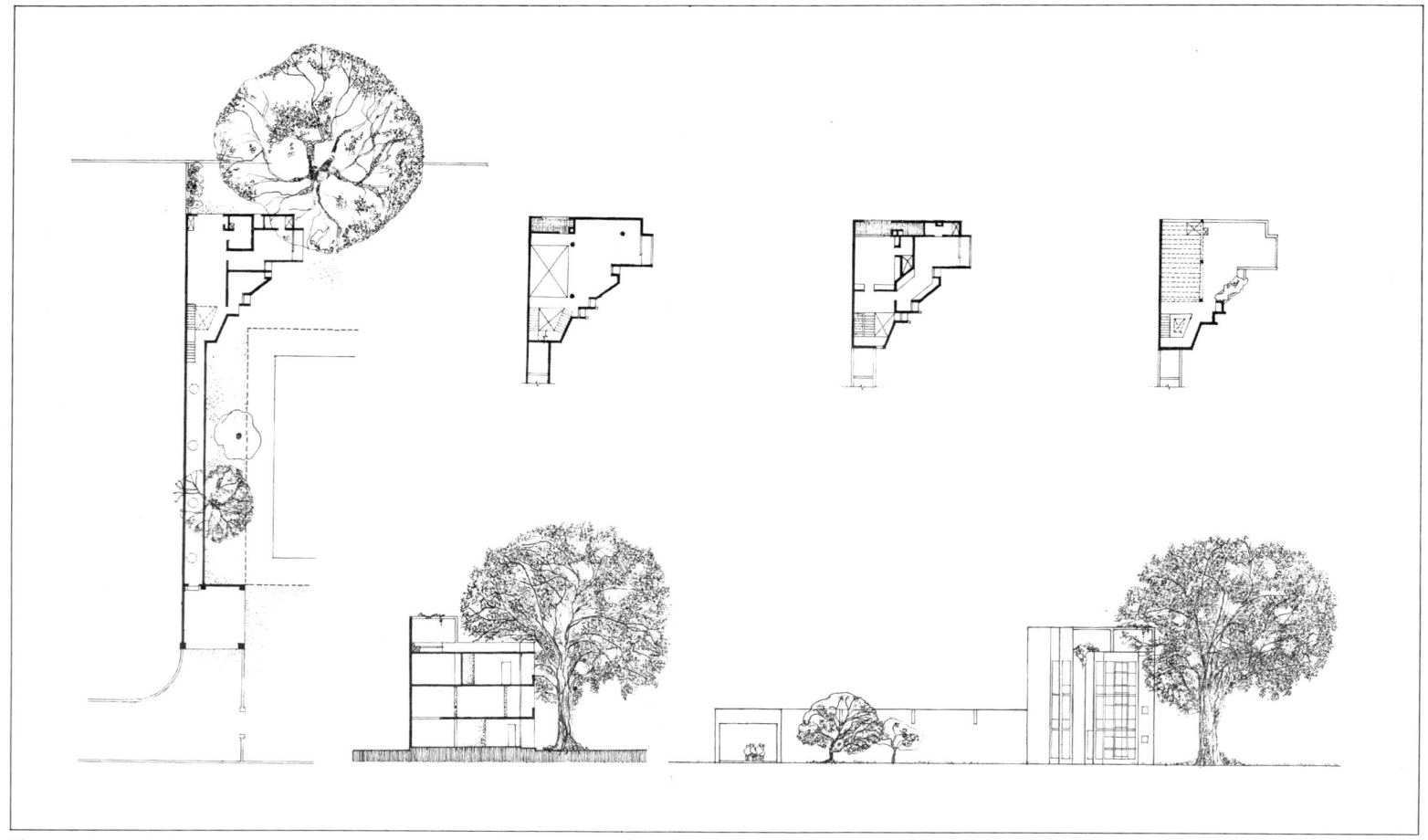

Plans, section and elevation. Martenstyn Tower.

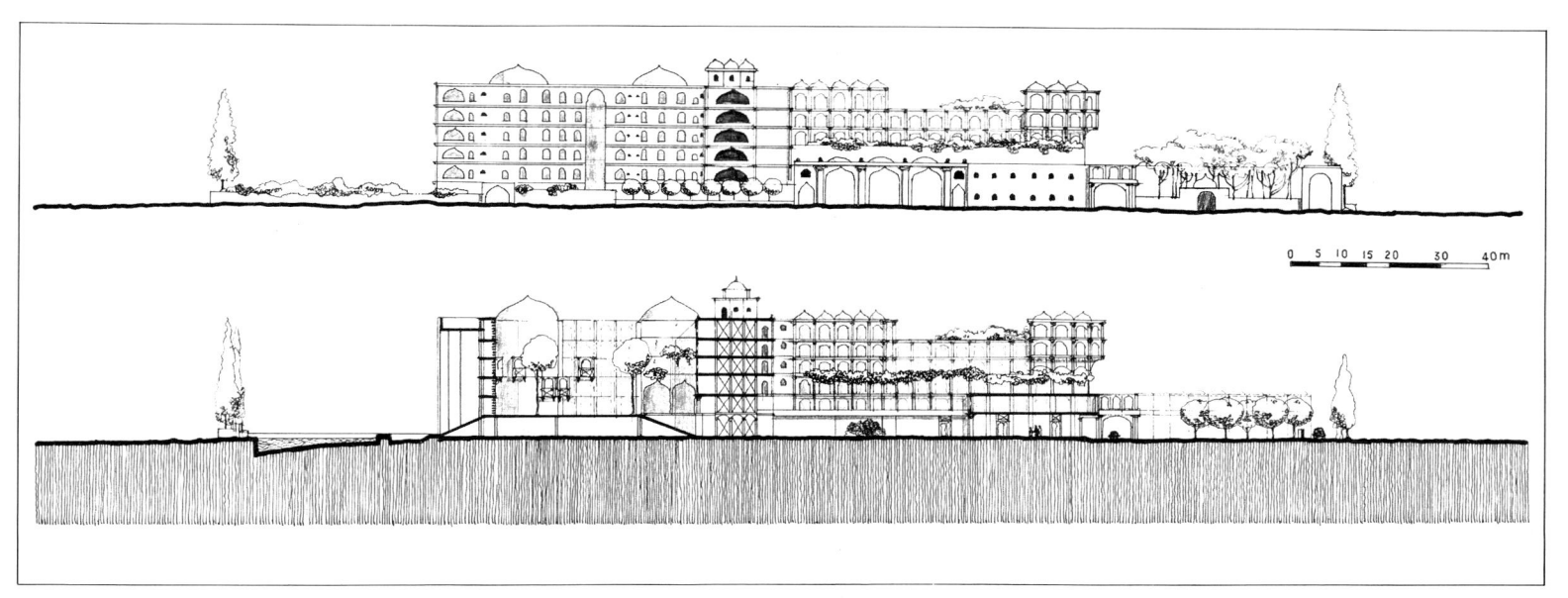

Section and elevation. Galadari Hotel.

INTERNATIONAL WINGED BEAN INSTITUTE, Pallekelle (designed).

1985

FITZHERBERT BROCKHOLES HOUSE, Tangalle.

L.R.P. DOSSA HOUSE, Kotte.

PHASE II: ARTS FACULTIES, LIBRARY, AND ADMINISTRATION BUILDING, Ruhunu University, Matara.

OFFICES FOR BANQUE INDOSUEZ, Colpetty, Colombo (designed).

ROYAL OCEANIC HOTEL, Negombo.

U.N. HEADQUARTERS, Malé, Maldives (designed).
Built on the atoll of Malé, the capital of the Maldives, the walls are structural and formed of white coral.

1987

DRUVI DE SARAM HOUSE 1
Ward Place, Colombo.

1988

EXTENSIONS TO INTEGRAL EDUCATION CENTRE, Piliyandala.

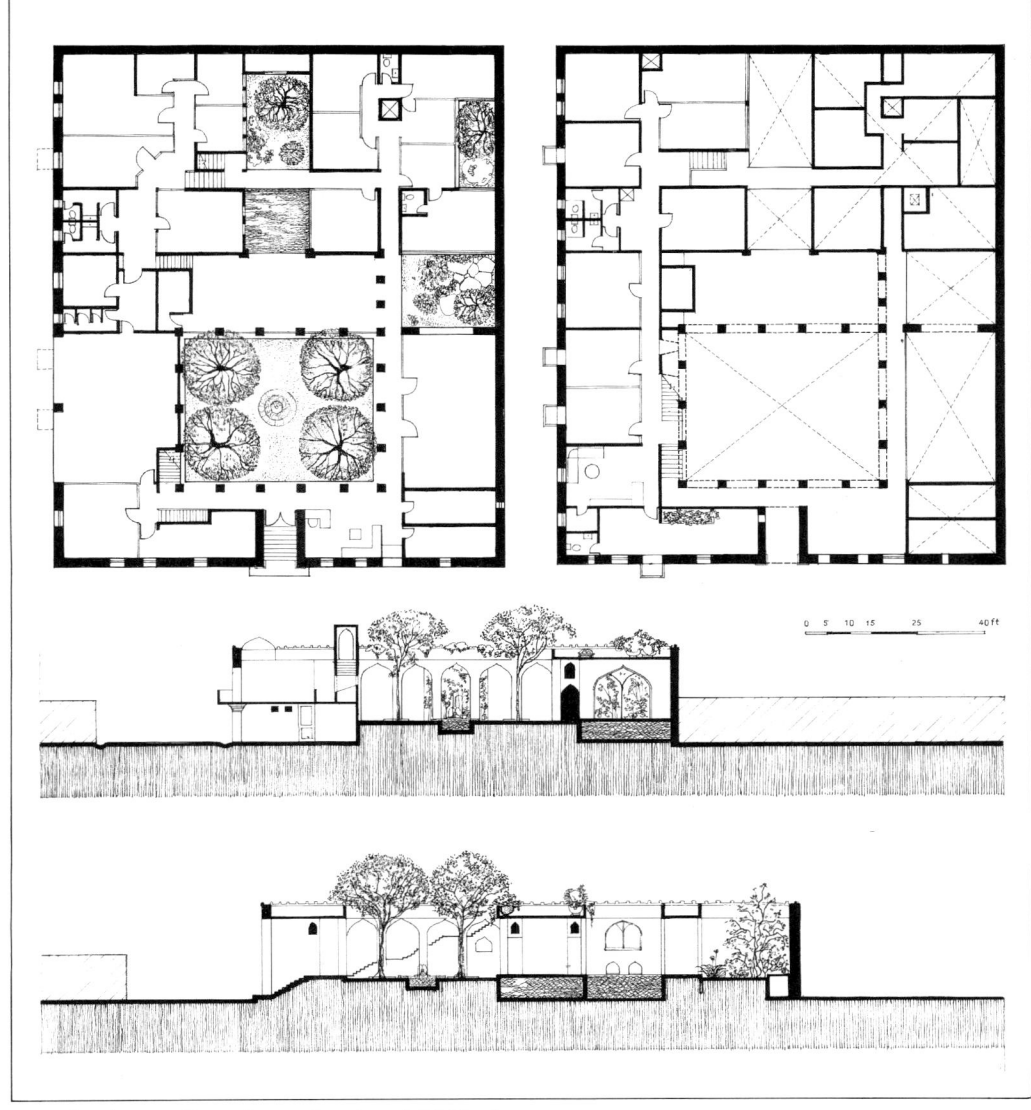

Ground and upper floor plans and sections. UN Headquarters.

1989

SINGAPORE CLOUD CENTRE,
BOTANICAL GARDENS, Singapore.
This was a project for a greenhouse to house vegetation from the mountains of Malaysia.

PARK ROYAL, SHERATON, Suva, Fiji (designed).

BALI HYATT EXTENSION, Bali (designed).

ALBERT TEO HOUSES,
Singapore (designed).

1990

DIAMOND BAY DEVELOPMENTS,
Penang, Malaysia (designed).

1991

BANYAN TREE RESORTS,
Bintan Island, Indonesia (designed).

1992

CITY DISPENSARY BUILDING,
Union Place, Colombo.

LARRY GORDON HOUSE, Wakaya, Fiji.

CHLOE DE SOYSA,
Dharmapala Mawatha, Colombo.

1993

MOWBRAY COUNTRY CLUB,
Kandy, Sri Lanka (designed).

HOUSE ON THE CINNAMON HILL,
Lunuganga, Bentota.

1994

KANDALAMA HOTEL, Dambulla, Sri Lanka.

SINDBAD GARDEN HOTEL,
Kalutara, Sri Lanka (under construction).

LIGHTHOUSE HOTEL,
Galle, Sri Lanka (under construction).

ORION HOTEL,
Ahungalla, Sri Lanka (designed).

DRUVI DE SARAM HOUSE 11,
Ward Place, Colombo (designed).

MODI HOUSE,
Dehra Mandi Village, Delhi, India (under construction).

CONVERSION OF CHICKA JHALLA FORT, Bangalore, India (under construction).

CURRUMJEE HOUSE, Curepipe, Mauritius.

ROHAN JAYAKODY HOUSE, Park Road, Colombo.

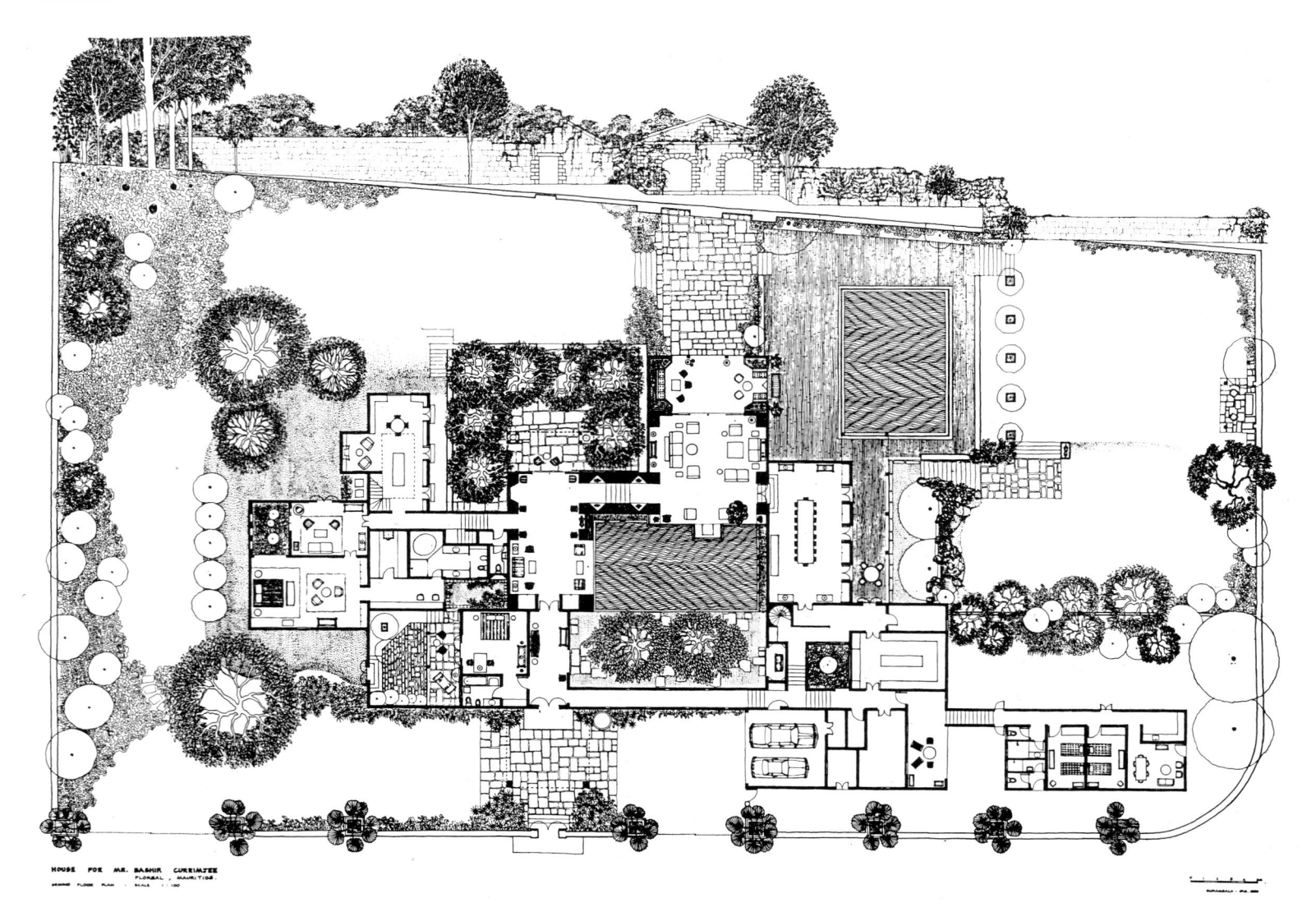

Currumjee House, Curepipe, Mauritius.

BIOGRAPHY

1919
Born in Colombo.

1941
Obtained Bachelor of Arts Degree (English Literature Tripos), Cambridge University, Cambridge.

1943
Admitted as Barrister-at-Law, Middle Temple, London.

1956
Received his Diploma in Architecture, The Architectural Association School, London.

1957
Associate, Royal Institute of British Architects.

1958
Partner, Edwards, Reid and Begg, Architects in Colombo.

1960
Associate, Sri Lanka Institute of Architects.

1967
Pan Pacific Architectural Citation from the Hawaii Chapter, American Institute of Architects.

1969
President, Sri Lanka Institute of Architects.

1982
Recipient of the Inaugural Gold Medal at the Silver Jubilee Celebrations of the Sri Lanka Institute of Architects.

1983
Pacific Area Travel Association (PATA) Heritage Award of Recognition for the New Parliament Complex at Sri Jayawardenepura, Kotte.

Honorary Fellow, American Institute of Architects.

1985
Conferred with the title 'Vidya Jothi' (Light of Science) in the inaugural Honours List of the President of Sri Lanka.

1986
Exhibition 'The Work of Geoffrey Bawa' presented by the Royal Institute of British Architects in London, and later exhibited in New York, Boston and Colombo.

Teaching Fellowship at the Aga Khan Programme for Architecture at MIT, Boston.

Reserve Judge at the International Competition for the Indira Gandhi Memorial, New Delhi.

Advisor to the Government of Fiji on the Restoration of the Old Capitol.

Guest Speaker at the second regional seminar of the Agha Khan Award for Architecture on 'Architects in Southern Asia', Dhaka, Bangladesh.

1987
Guest Speaker at the ARCASIA Forum on 'My Architecture', Bali, Indonesia.

1989
Member of the Master Jury for the Fourth Aga Khan Award for Architecture.

Guest Speaker at the PAM-SIA-CAA International Conference, 'Architecture and Tourism', Kuala Lumpur, Malaysia.

1990
Guest Speaker at the RAIA-PAM Conference, 'Architecture in Isolation', Perth, Australia and Kuala Lumpur, Malaysia.

1993
Conferred with the title 'Deshamanya' (Light of the Nation) in the Honours List of the President of Sri Lanka.

BIBLIOGRAPHY

The Architectural Review, "Ceylon - Seven new buildings", February 1966.

The Architectural Review, "Ceylon Pavilion at Expo '70", August 1970.

The Architectural Review, "Two Bawa", May 1983.

Architecture (USA), "Quietly Monumental Parliament Building in the new Capital City", September 1984.

Architecture (USA), "Gracefully horizontal university buildings overlooking the sea", September 1988.

Architecture Interior and Design (Australia), "Colombo - Bagatelle Road", January 1991.

Arradamento (Italy), December 1975.

"Batujimbar Bali", published by Geoffrey Bawa, 1976.

Bawa, Geoffrey and Plesnik, Ulrik, "Work in Ceylon", *Arkitekten* (Denmark), Nos. 16 and 17, 1965.

Bawa, Geoffrey, Bon, Christoph and Sansoni, Dominic, *Lunuganga*, Times Editions (Singapore), 1990.

Belle (Australia), "Sri Lanka: A sub-tropical retreat", May/June 1984.

Brace Taylor, Brian (with an essay by Barbara Sansoni), *Geoffrey Bawa*, Concept Media - Aperture, 1986.

Brawne, Michael, "The work of Geoffrey Bawa", *The Architectural Review*, April 1978.

Brawne, Michael, "From Idea to Building", Butterworth-Heinemann, 1992.

Brawne, Michael, "University of Ruhunu, Matara, Sri Lanka", *The Architectural Review*, November 1986.

de Silva, Caputo, "Sri Lanka - A house rich in local detail and nature", *Casa Vogue* (Italy), July/August 1993.

Fletcher, Sir Bannister, *History of Architecture*, 19th edition, Ed. Musgrove, John, Butterworth, 1987.

Jayawardene, Shanthee, "Bawa - A contribution to cultural regeneration", *Mimar 19*, January/March 1986.

Jayawardene, Shanthee, "Jewel of the Orient", *Building Design (UK)*, March 1986.

Laird, Simon, "Geoffrey Bawa and the architecture of Sri Lanka", *Mac II: The Magazine of the Mackintosh School of Architecture*, Scotland, 1984.

Lal, Ashok, "The Architecture of Geoffrey Bawa - An intimacy of experience and expression", *Architecture and Design* (India), Vol. 11, No. 2, March/April 1990.

Lewcock, Ronald, "Bawa - Arcadia in Sri Lanka", *RIBA Journal*, February 1986.

Articles by Lewcock, Ronald ("Profile: Geoffrey Bawa"); Ozkan, Suha ("On Geoffrey Bawa and Modesty in Architecture"); Robson, David ("The Architecture of Geoffrey Bawa") in *Arredamento Dekorasyon,* Sayi 38, Haziran 1992-

Lunuganga (Garden) featured in *The Landscape of Man* by Sir Geoffrey and Susan Jellicoe, Thames and Hudson,1987.

Majalah Arkitek (Malaysia), "Interview with Geoffrey Bawa", January/February 1990.

Mimar 25, "Club Villa, Bentota", September 1987.

Nakamura, Toshio, "The architecture of Geoffrey Bawa", *Architecture and Urbanism* (Japan), No. 141, June 1982.

Plesner, Ulrik, "A ten year old garden", *Arkitekten* (Denmark), 1959.

Powell, Robert, "Geoffrey Bawa - Seminal works in tropical architecture", *Singapore Institute of Architects Journal*, No. 143, July/August 1987.

Sabisch, Christine, "The Paradise is named Lunuganga", *Ambiente* (Germany), July/August 1992.

Serendib (Sri Lanka), "All roads will soon lead to Kotte", Vol. 3, No. 2, April/July 1984.

Serendib (Sri Lanka), "Sri Lanka's class structure", Vol. 6, No. 5, September/October 1987.

Richards, Sir James, "Geoffrey Bawa", *Mimar 19*, January/March 1986.

Ed. Richards, Sir James, *Who's Who in Architecture*, Weidenfeld and Nicolson, 1977.

Times of Ceylon Annual, "A way of building", 1968.

Viladas, Pilar, "This side of Paradise - Balinese elements accent a house in Fiji", *Architectural Digest* (USA), September 1994.

Walker Smith, Melissa, "Peace Plan" (featuring Donald Friend's Batujimbar Estate, Bali), *Belle* (Australia), February/March 1992.

The lagoon seen from the northern corner of the gravelled terrace.